The Polis
Bible Commentary

Volume 1a
Genesis 1-11

URBAN LOFT PUBLISHERS

The Polis
Bible Commentary

Volume 1a

Genesis 1-11

Biblical Exposition
John C. Nugent

Urban Ministry Commentary
Sean Benesh

Series Editor
Mark S. Krause

Senior Editor
Stephen E. Burris

URBAN LOFT PUBLISHERS

The Polis Bible Commentary: Genesis 1-11, Volume 1a

Copyright © 2018 by John Nugent

All rights reserved. Except for brief quotations in critical publications or reviews, no part of this book may be reproduced in any manner without prior written permission from the publisher.

Requests for information should be addressed to:

Urban Loft Publishers
6611 Aspen St.
La Vista, NE 68128

urbanloftpublishers.com

Stephen E. Burris, Senior Editor
Mark S. Krause, Series Editor

Scripture quotations are from New Revised Standard Version Bible, copyright © 1989 National Council of the Churches of Christ in the United States of America. Used by permission. All rights reserved worldwide.

ISBN: 978-1-949625-19-6

Cover picture: stairway of Mt. Sinai, Mark S. Krause

Table of Contents

Editor's Preface iii

Author's Preface iv

Bibliography v

An Introduction To Genesis 1-11 1
- A Missional Reading of Genesis 1
- Genesis and Cities 8
- Structure of Genesis 13
- Research Methodology 17

CREATION 1:1—2:25 18
Seven Day Creation: Genesis 1:1—2:3 18
- 1:1-2 In the Beginning 20
- 1:3—2:1 Six Days 22
- 2:2-3 Day Seven 29

Creation of Humans and Animals: Genesis 2:4-25 33
- 2:4-17 The Garden and the Human 33
- 2:18-25 The Human Needs a Counterpart 42

FALL AND AFTERMATH 3:1—6:4 48
Fall: 3:1-24 48
- 3:1-7 Creatures Conspire against God 48
- 3:8-24 Consequences for Disobedience 56

Aftermath of the Fall: Genesis 4:1—6:4 64
- 4:1-8 Brother Murders Brother 64
- 4:9-16 Consequences for Murder 70
- 4:17-26 Contrasting Legacies of Cain and Seth 73
- 5:1-32 Adam's Son to Noah's Sons 83
- 6:1-4 Sons of God 93

FLOOD AND AFTERMATH 6:5—11:32 108
Flood: 6:5—8:19 108
- The Flood and History 108
- The Flood and Ecology 110
- The Flood and Theology 111
- 6:5-13 God Resolves to Flood the Earth and Spare Noah 115
- 6:14—7:5 Noah Builds and Enters the Ark 120
- 7:6-24 Flood Waters Rise and Abate 123
- 8:1-19 God Remembers All His Creatures 124

Aftermath of Flood: 8:20—11:32 130
- 8:20-22 Noah's Altar and God's New Resolve 130
- 9:1-7 God's Blessing and New Restrictions 135
- 9:8-17 God's Covenant with All Creation 149
- 9:18-28 Noah's Cursed and Blessed Sons 152

10:1-32 The Dispersion of Noah's Sons 158
11:1-9 The Dispersion of Nimrod's Sons 168
11:10-26 Shem's Son to Terah's Sons 179
11:27-32 Terah's False Start 183

Genesis 1-11 and Mission 187

EDITOR'S PREFACE

This volume is part of an anticipated 30-volume set of commentaries for the entire Bible. Each volume will have Bible Exposition written by a capable Bible scholar and Urban Ministry Commentary sidebar insights written by an urban specialist. These urban insights will be marked with a shaded box and spread throughout the volume.

We have titled this series the ***Polis Bible Commentary***, using the Greek word πόλις (*polis*), the ancient designation for a city.

Ancient cities were centers for commerce, manufacturing, government, the arts, architecture, religious sites, and education. While the cities of Bible times had none of the technological features of modern cities, the difference between urban and rural settings was just as huge. Talent, ideas, and trends flowed to the urban centers from the rural world, with the urban influence coming back to rural residents with the city's stamp of influence.

This commentary series is written from the perspective that much of the Bible was written with cities in mind and intended for an urban audience. Urbanists today have taught us that the cities of our world have great similarities and commonalities as opposed to their surrounding rural areas. Missions endeavors originating in the Western churches have long targeted rural populations in Africa and Asia. Now, the demographic trends that are building the urban populations have turned this focus to cities. It is the desire of the authors and editors of this series that the intentional inclusion of an urban perspective will better serve those who serve and live in these dynamic cities.

John Nugent has taught at Great Lakes Christian College since 2002, now serving as Professor of Bible and Theology. Dr. Nugent's Ph.D. is from Calvin Theological Seminary. He is an ideal person to contribute to this series. He grew up on Long Island, NY and has a passion for conversing with fellow believers about God's mission in this world and the church's part in it.

Sean Benesh teaches at Warner Pacific University and other schools in the Portland, OR area. His doctorate is from Bakke Graduate University. He is the founder of Urban Loft Publishers and has several books under this imprint.

Mark S. Krause, August 2018

AUTHOR'S PREFACE

This commentary has been a pure joy to write, and I owe much of it to my teachers and students. The teacher who most opened my mind to the extraordinary world of Genesis is Paul J. Kissling. When I was a young college student, his advanced elective on Genesis was a turning point not only in my understanding of Genesis, but also in my ability to read Scripture critically, creatively, and missionally. A few degrees later, then as a colleague, I learned a great deal more from Paul when he invited me to proofread his insightful two-volume commentary on Genesis. The number of footnotes I've cited from his work hardly represents the degree to which my thought depends on his formal and informal instruction.

Having now taught several introductory and advanced courses on Genesis, I continue to learn from my own students. Their intellectual curiosity, probing questions, and passion for the abiding relevance of Scripture to the church's mission has prevented my own curiosity from ever waning. Though I am indebted to countless such students, I am especially inspired by those whose own research on Genesis has taught me much and received high honors in academic student paper competitions—students like Natasha Smith, Margaryta Teslina, and Josh Bush.

An overwhelming number of articles have been written on Genesis in recent years, so I am deeply grateful to Tommy Moehlman for combing through various databases and placing such research conveniently at my disposal. I would have struggled mightily to survey this vast literary landscape without him. I would also have failed to meet my deadline were it not for timely and careful readers like Branson Parler, Ted Troxell, Heather Bunce, Stephen Burris, and Mark Krause. Their work on this manuscript at different stages has strengthened it considerably.

Finally, I thank God daily for the constant love and support of my wife and best friend, Beth, our three daughters—Sierra, Alexia, and Alissa—and Delta Community Christian Church. Their ungrudging blessing to pursue such work on top of my full-time job and speaking engagements testifies to their self-giving commitment to God's kingdom.

John Nugent, July 2018

BIBLIOGRAPHY

Adamo, David Tuesday. "The Genesis Creation Accounts: An African Background." In *Genesis*. Texts @ Contexts Series, eds. Athalya Brenner, Archie Chi-chung Lee, and Gale A. Yee, 25-33. Minneapolis: Fortress, 2010.

Atwell, James E. "An Egyptian Source for Genesis 1." *Journal of Theological Studies* 51, pt. 2 (2000): 441-477.

Baden, Joel S. *The Composition of the Pentateuch: Renewing the Documentary Hypothesis*. New Haven: Yale University Press, 2012.

Bartholomew, Craig G. and Michael W. Goheen. *The Drama of Scripture: Finding Our Place in the Biblical Story*. Grand Rapids: Baker, 2004.

Beale, G. K. *The Temple and the Church's Mission: A Biblical Theology of the Dwelling Place of God*. New Studies in Biblical Theology 17. Downers Grove, IL: Intervarsity Press, 2004.

Bergsma, John Sietze and Scott Walker Hahn. "Noah's Nakedness and the Curse on Canaan (Genesis 9:20-27)." *Journal of Biblical Literature* 124 (2005): 25-40.

Berlyn, Patricia. "The Journey of Terah: To Ur-Kasdim or Urkesh?" *Jewish Biblical Quarterly* 33 (2005): 73-80.

Billings, Todd J. *The Word of God for the People of God: An Entry to the Theological Interpretation of Scripture*. Grand Rapids: Eerdmans, 2010.

Blumenthal, Fred. "Biblical Onomastics: What's in a Name." *Jewish Biblical Quarterly* 37 (2009): 124-128.

Boyd, Gregory A. *Crucifixion of the Warrior God: Interpreting the Old Testament's Violent Portraits of God in Light of the Cross*, vol. 2, *Cruciform Thesis*. Minneapolis, MN: Fortress, 2017.

Briggs, Richard S. "Humans in the Image of God and Other Things Genesis Does Not Make Clear." *Journal of Theological Interpretation* 4 (2010): 111-126.

Brodie, Thomas L. *Genesis As Dialogue: A Literary, Historical, & Theological Commentary*. Oxford: Oxford University Press, 2001.

Brown, William P. "Manifest Diversity: The Presence of God in Genesis." In *Genesis and Christian Theology*, eds. Nathan MacDonald, Mark W. Elliott, and Grant Macaskill, 3-25. Grand Rapids: Eerdmans, 2012.

Brueggemann, Walter. *Genesis*, Interpretation: A Bible Commentary for Teaching and Preaching. Atlanta: Westminster John Knox Press, 1982.

Cantz, Paul and Mirel Castle. "A Psycho-Biblical Response to Death Anxiety: Separation and Individuation Dynamics in the Babel Narrative." *Journal of Psychology & Theology* 41 (2013): 327-339.

Clark, Merilyn E. K. "A Flood of Justice: The Scope of Justice in the Flood Narrative (Gen. 6:5—9:19)." *International Journal of Public Theology* 3 (2009): 357-370.

Copan, Paul. *Is God a Moral Monster? Making Sense of the Old Testament God*. Grand Rapids: Baker, 2011.

Creach, Jerome F. D. *Violence in Scripture*. Interpretation: Resources for the Use of Scripture in the Church. Louisville, KY: Westminster John Knox Press, 2013.

Davies, Philip R. "And Enoch Was Not, For Genesis Took Him." In *Biblical Traditions in Transmission: Essays in Honour of Michael A. Knibb*, eds. Judith Lieu, Charlotte Hempel, Michael A. Knibb, 97-107. Leiden: Brill, 2006.

Dawkins, Richard. *The God Delusion*. Boston: Houghton Mifflin Company, 2006.

deClaissé-Walford, Nancy L. "Genesis 2: 'It is Not Good for the Human to Be Alone.'" *Review and Expositor* 103 (2006): 343-58.

_____. "God Came Down...and God Scattered: Acts of Punishment or Acts of Grace?" *Review and Expositor* 103 (2006): 403-417.

Dershowitz, Alan. *The Genesis of Justice: Ten Stories of Biblical Injustice that Led to the Ten Commandments and Modern Law.* New York: Warner Books, 2000.

Embry, Brad. "The 'Naked Narrative' from Noah to Leviticus: Reassessing Voyeurism in the Account of Noah's Nakedness in Genesis 9.22-24." *Journal for the Study of the Old Testament* 35 (2011): 417-433.

Eslinger, Lyle. "The Enigmatic Plurals like 'One of Us' (Genesis I 26, III 22, and XI 7) in Hyperchronic Perspective." *Vetus Testamentum* 56 (2006): 172-184.

Farkas, David S. "In Search of the Biblical Hammurabi." *Jewish Biblical Quarterly* 39 (2011): 159-164.

Fekkes, Jan. *Isaiah and Prophetic Traditions in the Book of Revelation: Visionary Antecedents and their Development.* Journal for the study of the New Testament Supplement series 93. Sheffield, England: JSOT Press, 1994.

Fenton, Terry. "Nimrod's Cities: An Item from the Rolling Corpus." In *Genesis, Isaiah and Psalms: A Festschrift to honour Professor John Emerton for his Eightieth Birthday*, eds. Katherine J. Dell, Graham Davies, and Yee Von Koh, 23-31. Boston: Brill, 2010.

Fouts, David M. "Peleg in Gen 10:25." *Journal of the Evangelical Theological Society* 41 (1998): 17-21.

Fretheim, Terence E. "The God of the Flood Story and Natural Disasters." *Calvin Theological Journal* 43 (2008): 21-34.

Friedman, Richard Elliott. *The Bible with Sources Revealed: A New View into the Five Books of Moses.* New York: HarperOne, 2003.

Grundke, Christopher L. K. "A Tempest in a Teapot? Genesis III 8 Again." *Vetus Testamentum* 51 (2001): 548-551.

Hallow, William W. and K. Lawson Younger, eds. *The Context of Scripture*. Vol. 1. Leiden: Brill, 2002.

Hamilton, Victor P. *The Book of Genesis: Chapters 1-17*. The New International Commentary on the Old Testament. Grand Rapids: Eerdmans, 1990.

Hauerwas, Stanley. *With the Grain of the Universe: The Church's Witness and Natural Theology*. Grand Rapids: Baker, 2001.

Hepner, Gershon. "The Depravity of Ham and the Tower of Babel Echo Contiguous Laws of the Holiness Code." *Estudios Biblicos* 61 (2003): 85-131.

Herman, Steward W. "On Primal Fear and Confidence: Reinterpreting the Myth of the Flood as the Climate Changes." *Word & World* 29 (2009): 63-74.

Hiebert, Theodore. "The Tower of Babel and the Origin of the World's Cultures." *Journal of Biblical Literature* 126 (2007): 29-58.

Hill, Carol A. "Making Sense of the Numbers of Genesis." *Perspectives on Science and Christian Faith: Journal of the American Scientific Affiliation* 55 (2003): 239-251.

Hinckly Jr., Robert M. "Adam, Aaron, and the Garden Sanctuary." *Logia* 4 (2013): 5-12.

Hom, Mary Katherine Y. H. "'...A Mighty Hunter before YHWH': Genesis 10:9 and the Moral-Theological Evaluation of Nimrod." *Vetus Testamentum* 60 (2010): 63-68.

House, Wayne and John Howard Yoder. *The Death Penalty Debate*. Dallas: Word Publishing, 1991.

Hurowitz, Victor Avigdor. "In Search of Resen (Genesis 10:12): Dur-Sarrukin?" In *Birkat Shalom: Studies in the Bible, Ancient Near Eastern Literature, and Postbiblical Judaism; Present to Shalom M. Paul on* the Occasion of his Seventieth Birthday, ed. Chaim Cohen, 511-524. Winona Lake, IN: Eisenbrauns: 2008.

Johnston, Gordon H. "Genesis 1 and Ancient Egyptian Creation Myths." *Bibliotheca Sacra* 165 (2008): 178-94.

Kawashima, Robert S. "*Homer Faber* in J's Primeval History." *Zeitschrift fur die alttestamentliche Wissenschaft* 116 (2004): 483-501.

Keiter, Sheila Tuller. "Outsmarting God: Egyptian Slavery and the Tower of Babel." *Jewish Biblical Quarterly* 41 (2013): 200-204.

Keller, Catherine. "'Be This Fish': A Theology of Creation out of Chaos." *Word & World* 32 (2012): 15-20.

Kissling, Paul J. *Genesis*. The College Press NIV Commentary. Vol. 1. Joplin, MO: College Press, 2004.

_____. *Genesis*. The College Press NIV Commentary. Vol. 2. Joplin, MO: College Press, 2009.

_____. "The Rainbow in Genesis 9:12-17: A Triple Entendre?" *Stone-Campbell Journal* 4 (2001): 249-261.

Knohl, Israel. "Nimrod, Son of Cush, King of Mesopotamia and the Dates of P and J." In *Birkat Shalom: Studies in the Bible, Ancient Near Eastern Literature, and Postbiblical Judaism; Present to Shalom M. Paul on the Occasion of his Seventieth Birthday*, ed. Chaim Cohen, 45-52. Winona Lake, IN: Eisenbrauns: 2008.

Kreider, Glenn R. "The Flood is as Bad as It Gets: Never Again Will God Destroy the Earth." *Bibliotheca Sacra* 171 (2014): 418-439.

Lacocque, André. "Whatever Happened in the Valley of Shinar? A Response to Theodore Hiebert." *Journal of Biblical Literature* 128 (2009): 29-41.

Levin, Yigal. "Nimrod the Mighty, King of Kish, King of Sumer and Akkad." *Vetus Testamentum* 52 (2002): 350-366.

Lim, Johnson Teng Kok. "Explication of an Exegetical Enigma in Genesis 1:1-3." *The Asia Journal of Theology* 16, no. 2 (Oct 2002): 301-314.

──────. "Genesis 1-11 and its Ancient Near Eastern Parallels." *The Asia Journal of Theology* 19, vol. 1 (2005): 68-78.

Luther, Martin. "Secular Authority: To What Extent It Should Be Obeyed." In *Martin Luther: Selections from his Writings*, ed. John Dillenberger, 363-402. New York: Doubleday, 1962.

Kvanvig, Helge S. "Gen 6, 1-4 as an Antediluvian Event." *Scandinavian Journal of the Old Testament* 16, no. 1 (2002): 79-112.

Jeon, Jeong Koo. "The Noahic *Covenants* and the Kingdom of God." *Mid-America Journal of Theology* 24 (2013): 179-209.

Litke, Joel. "The Message of Chapter 4 of Genesis." *Jewish Biblical Quarterly* 31 (2003): 197-200.

Löwisch, Ingeborg. "Gender and Ambiguity in the Genesis Genealogies: Tracing Absence and Subversion Through the Lens of Derrida's Archive Fever." In *Embroidered Garments: Priests and Gender in Biblical Israel*, ed. Deborah W. Rooke, 60-73. Sheffield: Sheffield Phoenix Press, 2009.

Maller, Allen S. "The City of Babel and Its Tower." *Jewish Biblical Quarterly* 40 (2012): 171-173.

Mason, Steven D. "Another Flood? Genesis 9 and Isaiah's Broken Eternal Covenant." *Journal for the Study of the Old Testament* 32 (2007): 177-98.

McKinlay, Judith E. "Bothering to Enter the Garden of Eden Once Again." *Feminist Theology* 19 (2010): 143-153.

Mellinkoff, Ruth. *The Mark of Cain*. Berkeley, CA: University of California Press, 1981.

Moberly, R. W. L. "The Mark of Cain – Revealed at Last." *Harvard Theology Review* 100 (2007): 11-28.

Middleton, J. Richard. *The Liberating Image: The Imago Dei in Genesis One.* Grand Rapids: Brazos Press, 2005.

_____. *A New Heaven and a New Earth: Reclaiming Biblical Eschatology.* Grand Rapids: Baker, 2014.

Moskala, Jiří. "Interpretation of $b^e re'\v{s}ît$ in the Context of Genesis 1:1-3." *Andrews University Seminary Studies* 49 (2011): 33-44.

Moyaert, Marianne. "A 'Babelish' World (Genesis 11:1-9) and its Challenge to Cultural-Linguistic Theory." *Horizons* 36 (2009): 215-34.

Muhly, James. "How Iron Technology Changed the Ancient World and Gave the Philistines a Military Edge." *Biblical Archaeology Review* 8 (1982): 40-54.

Niehaus, Jeffrey. "In the Wind of the Storm." *Vetus Testamentum* XLIV (1994): 263-267.

Nugent, John C. "Beyond Pacifism and Militarism: A Canonical Approach to Christians and Warfare." *Stone-Campbell Journal* 19 (2016): 205-217.

_____. *Endangered Gospel: How Fixing the World is Killing the Church.* Eugene, OR: Cascade Books, 2016.

_____. *The Politics of Yahweh: John Howard Yoder, the Old Testament, and the People of God.* Eugene, OR: Cascade Books, 2011.

Odhiambo, Nicholas. "The Nature of Ham's Sin." *Bibliotheca Sacra* 170 (2013): 154-65.

Parler, Branson. *Things Hold Together: John Howard Yoder's Trinitarian Theology of Culture.* Harrisonburg, VA: Herald Press, 2012.

Penley, Paul T. "A Historical Reading of Genesis 11:1-9: The Sumerian Demise and Dispersion Under the UR III Dynasty." *Journal of the Evangelical Theological Society* 50 (2007): 693-714.

Pinker, Aron. "Nimrod Found?" *Jewish Biblical Quarterly* 26 (1998): 237-245.

Pleins, J. David. *When the Great Abyss Opened: Classic and Contemporary Readings of Noah's Flood*. New York: Oxford University Press, 2003.

Rogland, Max. "Interpreting את in Genesis 2.5-6: Neglected Rabbinic and Intertextual Evidence." *Journal for the Study of the Old Testament* 34 (2010): 379-93.

Ron, Zvi. "The Book of Jubilees and the Midrash Part 3: The Tower of Babel." *Jewish Bible Quarterly* 42 (2014): 165-168.

Routledge, Robin L. "'My spirit' in Genesis 1-4." *Journal of Pentecostal Theology* 20 (2011): 232-251.

Sanneh, Lamin. *Translating the Message: The Missionary Impact on Culture*. Marynoll, NY: Orbis Books, 1989.

Schachter, Lifsa Block. "The Garden of Eden as God's First Sanctuary." *Jewish Bible Quarterly* 41 (2013): 73-77.

Schatz, Elihu A. "Sons of Elokim as used in Genesis." *Jewish Bible Quarterly* 36 (2008): 125-26.

Scotchmer, Paul F. "Lessons from Paradise on Work, Marriage, and Freedom: A Study of Genesis 2:4-3:24." *Evangelical Review of Theology* 28 (2004): 80-85.

Seeley, Paul H. "The Date of the Tower of Babel and Some Theological Implications." *Westminster Theological Journal* 63 (2001): 15-38.

_____. "Noah's Flood: Its Date, Extent, and Divine Accommodation." *Westminster Theological Journal* 66 (2004): 291-311.

Shemesh, Yael. "Vegetarian Ideology in Talmuidic Literature and Traditional Biblical Exegesis." In *Genesis*, Texts @ Contexts Series, eds. Athalya Brenner, Archie Chi-chung Lee, and Gale A. Yee, 107-127. Minneapolis: Fortress, 2010.

Sherwin, Byron L. "The Tower of Babel in Eliezer Ashkenazi's *Sefer Ma'aseh Hashem*." *Jewish Biblical Quarterly* 42 (2014): 83-88.

Snyder, Graydon F. and Kenneth M. Shaffer. "On Racism." *Brethren Life & Thought* (2009): 55-60.

Spero, Shubert. "Sons of God, Daughters of Men?" *Jewish Bible Quarterly* 40 (2012): 15-18.

Stone, Lawson G. "The Soul: Possession, Part, or Person?" In *What About the Soul: Neuroscience and Christian Anthropology*, ed. Joel B. Green, 47-61. Nashville: Abingdon, 2004.

Strong, John T. "Shattering the Image of God: A Response to Theodore Hiebert's Interpretation of the Story of the Tower of Babel." *Journal of Biblical Literature* 127 (2008): 625-634.

Sunquist, Scott. *Understanding Christian Mission: Participation in Suffering and Glory*. Grand Rapids: Baker, 2013.

Toorn, K. van der and P. W. van der Horst. "Nimrod Before and After the Bible." *Harvard Theological Review* 83 (1990): 1-29.

Treier, Daniel J. *Introducing Theological Interpretation of Scripture: Recovering a Christian Practice*. Grand Rapids: Baker, 2008.

VanDrunen, David. "Natural Law in Noahic Accent: A Covenantal Conception of Natural Law Drawn from Genesis 9." *Journal of the Society of Christian Ethics* 30 (2010): 131-49.

_____. "The Protectionist Purpose of Law: A Moral Case from the Biblical Covenant with Noah." *Journal of the Society of Christian Ethics* 35 (2015): 101-117.

Walker-Jones, Arthur. "Eden for Cyborgs: Ecocriticism and Genesis 2-3." *Biblical Interpretation* 16 (2008): 263-293.

Walton, John H. "Creation in Genesis 1:1-2:3 and the Ancient Near East: Order out of Disorder after *Chaoskampt*." *Calvin Theological Journal* 43 (2008): 48-63.

_____. *The Lost World of Genesis One: Ancient Cosmology and the Origins Debate.* Downers Grove, IL: InterVarsity Press, 2009.

Weaver, J. Denny. *The Nonviolent God.* Grand Rapids: Eerdmans, 2013.

Whitekettle, Richard. "Freedom from Fear and Bloodshed: Hosea 2.20 (Eng. 18) and the End of Human/Animal Conflict." *Journal for the Study of the Old Testament* 37 (2012): 219-236.

Wilkinson, David. "Reading Genesis 1-3 in the Light of Modern Science." In *Reading Genesis after Darwin*, eds. Stephen C. Barton and David Wilkinson, 127-144. Oxford University Press, 2009.

Wittenberg, Gunther. "Alienation and 'Emancipation' from the Earth: The Earth Story in Genesis 4." In *The Earth Story in Genesis*, eds. Norman C. Habel and Shirley Wurst, 105-116. Sheffield: Sheffield Academic Press, 2000.

Wright, Christopher J. H. *The Mission of God: Unlocking the Bible's Grand Narrative.* Downers Grove, IL: InterVarsity, 2006.

Yamauchi, Edwin M. "The Curse of Ham." *Criswell Theological Review* 6 (2009): 45-60.

Yoder, John Howard. *The End of Sacrifice: The Capital Punishment Writings of John Howard Yoder*, ed. John C. Nugent. Harrisonburg, VA: Herald Press, 2011.

_____. "Feminist Theology Miscellany #1: Salvation Through Mothering?" April 1988. Available in the John Howard Yoder Digital Library at http://palni.contentdm.oclc.org/cdm/landingpage/collection/p15705coll18.

_____. "On Generating Alternative Paradigms." In *Human Values and the Environment: Conference Proceedings* no. 140, 57-59. Madison, WI: Wisconsin Academy of Science, Arts, and Letters, 1992.

---------. *Preface to Theology: Christology and Theological Method*, eds. Stanley Hauerwas and Alex Sider. Grand Rapids: Brazos Press, 2002.

---------. *Theology of Mission: A Believers Church Perspective*, eds. Gayle Gerber Koontz and Andy Alexis-Baker. Downers Grove, IL: IVP Academic, 2014.

Young, Dwight Wayne. "The Step-down to Two Hundred in Genesis 11, 10-25." *Zeitschrift für die alttestamentliche Wissenschaft* 116 (2004): 323-333.

Zevit, Ziony. "Was Eve Made from Adam's Rib—or His Baculum." *Biblical Archaeology Review* 41 (Sept/Oct 2015): 33-35.

---------. *What Really Happened in the Garden of Eden*. New Haven, CT: Yale University Press, 2013.

AN INTRODUCTION TO GENESIS 1-11

A Missional Reading of Genesis

This commentary offers a missional reading of Genesis. Since the term "missional" means different things to different people, it is necessary to clarify what we do and do not mean by it. We do not consider "missional" a specific method for interpreting Scripture; it is more of an aim or a sensibility. That being the case, its proponents are likely to use a wide variety of interpretive approaches and may benefit greatly from them.

We could, for instance, focus on exegesis of the original language of Genesis, the composition of Genesis, the sources behind Genesis, any redactors that were involved in shaping the text, and whatever ancient Near Eastern literature may have influenced them. All these efforts could draw us closer to a truly contextual reading – none of the information learned would go to waste. Yet the purpose of this series, its target audience, and word limits require us to focus more on some things than on others. We will use footnotes to refer readers to sources for further research in areas that get less emphasis.

In keeping with the design of this series, we work primarily with the final form of Genesis as preserved in the NRSV. We operate under the assumption that the text as we have it, arranged precisely how it is, reflects the original intent of the canonical author or editor. Still we acknowledge that if some versions of source criticism are right, we risk connecting dots that neither the original authors, sources, redactors, or even God intended. This places us somewhere in the ballpark of both theological interpreters of Scripture and biblical studies specialists.[1] Even though we do not offer an original translation of the Hebrew text, we conduct our reading with the Hebrew Bible in hand and draw attention to places where the original language makes a significant contribution to a missional reading.

We also pay attention to how ancient Near Eastern background specialists contribute to our understanding of Genesis. We do so because we believe that a missional or theological interpretation of Scripture is not extraneous to the original text. Put differently, Scripture on its own terms and in its original context is already a missional document. Even if its original authors did not grasp the full scope of that mission, the faith community that brought these books into existence was playing an important part in God's mission. They were composing, preserving, arranging, editing, and compiling a key witness to God's saving acts in world history.

It is tempting to say that Genesis, indeed most of the Old Testament, is not a missionary document. After all, most of its authors thought they were simply preserving their family history. They thought they were special by virtue of being chosen as God's holy people, and they may never have thought they would become missionaries to the Gentiles as we think of mission. It is common for scholars to undercut the missionary impulse of Genesis by observing that its key missionary passage, "You will be a blessing to all nations" (Gen 12:1-3), is more properly translated as "all nations will bless themselves by you." Thus, the Israelites did not view themselves as "go ye therefore" type missionaries but as people with their own localized agenda. It is only by their own initiative that Gentiles would find a way to capitalize on Israel's prosperity. This is supported by other Old Testament passages that envision the nations streaming to Israel,

---

[1] See Daniel J. Treier, *Introducing Theological Interpretation of Scripture: Recovering a Christian Practice* (Grand Rapids: Baker Academic, 2008); and Todd J. Billings, *The Word of God for the People of God: An Entry to the Theological Interpretation of Scripture* (Grand Rapids: Eerdmans, 2010).

learning God's ways, and then returning home (Isa 2:3; Mic 4:1-2).

This line of interpretation presupposes a narrow view of God's missionary people. It assumes that mission work is inherently *centrifugal* in nature—that is, that proper missionary movement always emanates from the center until it reaches the outermost regions. Genesis and the Old Testament in general, however, exhibit a *centripetal* movement that prevents objects from drifting away by keeping them close to the center. God's people are at their best when they strive to keep separate from the nations and at their worst when they mingle with them. This being the case, it appears as if the Old Testament cannot truly be a missionary document.

Though this interpretation has some merit, if one presupposes that the Bible presents a coherent story with movement and direction, then it becomes clear that God's mission has both centripetal and centrifugal moments. When parenting, there is a time for keeping children safe at home and a time for sending them out into the world. Also, in parenting, there are times early on when children do not fully grasp the future freedom and mobility that awaits them. Such is the case with Israel. Scripture preserves the partial realization of God's people during different phases of their formation for mission.

Taken as a whole, the Bible culminates in the church carrying forth God's mission all throughout the world. But God's people did not and could not have started out that way. They started small—with one man, Abram, and his wife, Sarai. From this modest beginning, their missional identity unfolded in at least four phases:

1. They had to become a numerous people with a distinct identity;

2. They had to become a numerous people with a distinct identity that reflects God's intentions for all creation;

3. They had to become a numerous people with a distinct identity that reflects God's intentions for all creation

and is scattered throughout the world and therefore positioned to bless the world;

4. They had to become a numerous people with a distinct identity that reflects God's intentions for all creation and is scattered throughout the world and therefore positioned to bless the world by the power of God's Spirit, having been redeemed, reconciled, and restored by God's son, Jesus.

It is customary to identify only the fourth and final phase with God's mission. Yet this phase is not possible without the previous three, which it presupposes. They are all integral to God's mission, and we cannot not fully grasp phase four without understanding God's long and patient work in phases one through three.

In light of this wider biblical trajectory, we can begin to grasp what a missional reading of Genesis might entail. It may not contain the whole mission, but Genesis represents the backstory to the mission and its initial beginnings. In particular, Genesis 1-11 discusses why God needed to form a people with a distinct identity that reflects God's intention for all creation, and Genesis 12-50 discusses how God began to form that people.

Since God's mission in this world requires the active participation of a people, the formation, backstory, and self-understanding of that people is critical to God's mission. This is especially so because the identity of God's people is tied to their mission and not incidental to it. For example, if the mission of an organization is to put flyers in every mailbox within a mile radius of a given business from 9AM to 5PM, Monday through Friday, then the diet, sexual practices, and recreational habits of its workers over the weekend may not matter much to the fulfillment of their mission. As long as they show up each weekday and carry out the assignment with excellence, their employers will likely be pleased. This changes when the mission itself requires its missionaries to be a specific kind of people, which is certainly the case within the Bible story.[2] To understand the truth of this maxim and its relevance to a missional reading of Genesis, we need to understand why it is important to the biblical story that the identity of God's people reflects God's intentions for all creation.

The easy answer to this question is that, according to Genesis 1-11, God's original intentions for creation were severely compromised by sin. But that is not enough. We must add that God's primary strategy in Scripture for overcoming the disastrous consequences of sin is to use a people as a witness, role model, and demonstration plot of how rightly ordered creation functions. God is not simply using a people to *tell* others what he wants from them; God is using a people to *show* others what he wants from them. And Scripture makes quite clear that God has little use for *telling* that is divorced from *showing* (e.g., Jas 2:16).

Most believers are familiar with New Testament statements to this effect. Jesus begins the Sermon on the Mount by reminding his followers that they are called to be bright light and savory salt and that failure to be so renders them useless for God's purposes (Matt 5:13-15). Jesus did not pioneer this image. Hundreds of years earlier, when the Israelites were undergoing the identity crisis imposed upon them by the exile, the prophet of Isaiah 49 instructs God's people that they will not have the kind of power required to right the ship of world history. They will be powerless to punish the ruthless Babylonians and to restore those Israelites that Babylon had devastated.

That poses no problems, however, because God had already announced that the Persian ruler, Cyrus, would accomplish this task (Isa 44:24-28; 45:1-7, 13). Indeed, any powerful world leader can be used by God to keep in check other world rulers who abuse their power. Likewise, any wealthy royal benefactor can finance the Israelites' return from exile and rebuilding of Jerusalem's temple and city

---

[2] John Howard Yoder, *Theology of Mission: A Believers Church Perspective*, edited by Gayle Gerber Koontz and Andy Alexis-Baker (Downers Grove, IL: IVP Academic, 2014), 57.

walls. Leaving these important tasks in the hands of God and Persia, the prophet reminds the Israelites of their higher calling, saying, "It is too light a thing that you should be my servant to raise up the tribes of Jacob and to restore the survivors of Israel; I will give you as a light to the nations, that my salvation may reach to the end of the earth" (Isa 49:6). Persians cannot do that; only a numerous people with a distinct identity that reflects God's intentions for all creation can do that.

Still this vision of Isaiah has deeper roots. When Jesus stood on a mountain and called his followers to be savory salt and bright light, he was echoing Moses' famous mountain speech in Deuteronomy 4:

> See, just as the LORD my God has charged me, I now teach you statutes and ordinances for you to observe in the land that you are about to enter and occupy. You must observe them diligently, for this will show your wisdom and discernment to the peoples, who, when they hear all these statutes, will say, "Surely this great nation is a wise and discerning people!" For what other great nation has a god so near to it as the LORD our God is whenever we call to him? And what other great nation has statutes and ordinances as just as this entire law that I am setting before you today? (Deut 4:5-8)

God did not call the Israelites to obey Torah in order that they might stay on his good side, earn their salvation, or come to grips with their inadequacies and need for a savior. Rather, God called Abraham's descendants to live out Torah so the nations might catch a glimpse of God's good intentions for creation and might be drawn to God through their witness and example.

This may be why, immediately after delivering them from Egypt, the first thing God has Moses tell the Israelites is that they are "a priestly kingdom and a holy nation" (Exod 19:6). Though the whole earth belongs to its creator, God's people are set apart in a manner analogous to priests. This image can mean many things, but since it is given to the

Israelites who would soon receive divine blueprints for their own priesthood, it should at least mean that they will function for the nations like their own priests functioned for them.

Since Israel's priests did many things, it is somewhat unfortunate that they are mostly remembered for their role in the sacrificial cult. The Aaronic priests who served this function constituted but a small sampling of the wider group of Levites who served God's people in priestly ways. Other Levites hosted cities of refuge to protect innocent and guilty slayers, exemplified what it means to live as guests in the land of others and, perhaps most importantly, became Torah experts who could instruct Israel's tribes as to the common life to which God has called them as a witness to the nations (Deut 17:18; 31:9; 33:8-10).

The first task of God's people is to conform their life to God's intentions because that is how they accomplish their role in God's mission. Since their specific identity is central, the book that lays the foundation for it—Torah as a whole and Genesis more specifically—is of vital missional importance. This is so regardless of whether Genesis was written by Moses in the 14th-13th centuries BCE or by a priestly or non-priestly editor, compiler, or preservationist in the 6th century.

A missional approach to Genesis, or any other Bible book, does not mean using or not using a particular hermeneutical method. Rather, it means interpreting Genesis as part of God's wider mission that spans the entirety of Scripture. It presumes that God's mission is central to the biblical canon, and it uses whatever interpretive techniques shed light on that mission. It need not read God's mission into every passage regardless of whether it is already there, for it operates with the conviction that each passage on its own terms is already part of the wider missionary fabric of Scripture.

Genesis and Cities

One of the aims of this commentary series is to bring the insights of Scripture to bear on the urban mission context. To do so we have chosen to identify the urban context of each Bible book. Genesis is tricky in this regard because scholars have not been able to agree upon the authorship, location, and time of Genesis.

If Moses wrote Genesis in its entirety, which few scholars believe today, then he did so as a man without a city. He left behind the high civilization of Egypt as a young man and came to dwell among the tents of Midian before encountering God in the burning bush. After that encounter, he wandered alongside the Israelites until his death. If multiple sources were involved in the composition of Genesis, which is more likely, then we are dealing with a long and complicated history of oral and written transmission of the various sources, each with its own unique back story. Then we have to determine who, where, when, and how the final form of the Pentateuch came into being. If we had this information, we could at least sketch the urban landscape of the final editor and original audience of the canonical form of Genesis. Theories concerning multiple sources have been advanced under the rubric of the "documentary hypothesis."[3] This theory holds that the Pentateuch was composed from at least four primary sources:

1. A Yahwist source (J) originally identified with 850 BCE, but later adjusted to 960 – 930 BCE. This source would have been associated with a united Davidic Kingdom and would have been closely associated with Jerusalem.

2. An Elohist source (E), which was associated with the Northern Kingdom after the collapse of the united

---

[3] For a helpful introduction to the documentary hypothesis, see Joel S. Baden, *The Composition of the Pentateuch: Renewing the Documentary Hypothesis* (New Haven: Yale University Press, 2012).

monarchy. It would have been written around 850 BCE and would have had closer ties to the North's capital city, Samaria.

3. A Deuteronomist source (D) could have been written as early as 850 BCE, but no later than 620 BCE since portions of it seem to have been instrumental in Josiah's reforms at that time. If an early date holds, then it would have originated in the Northern Kingdom, like E. If a later date, after 721/22 BCE, then the destruction of Samaria would suggest a different urban context.

4. A Priestly source (P) is traditionally dated around 550-450 BCE, over a century after the fall of Jerusalem and the Southern Kingdom. This late date would mean that the Israelites would have had fresh firsthand experience of various cities to which they were exiled. It would also mean that their own capital, Jerusalem, had been reduced to a province of a foreign empire, whether Babylon before 539 BCE or Persia after 539 BCE.

Since D pertains to Deuteronomy alone, this Genesis commentary would only be concerned with J, E, and P.[4] This would give us a compositional history spanning five centuries (10th – 6th BCE), three different variations of the Israelite Kingdom (united, divided, and subjugated), and the influence of four different foreign empires (Assyria, Egypt, Babylon, and Persia).

The Documentary Hypothesis only complicates our search for a single urban context for Genesis. First, it furnishes no single context, but a plurality of contexts. Second, it has come under serious scrutiny by scholars. Some call into question the way it splits up the text and argue for literary readings that point to a stronger sense of unity.[5] Others

---

[4] For a recent statement of what passages in Genesis are traditionally associated with what sources, see Richard Elliott Friedman, *The Bible with Sources Revealed: A New View into the Five Books of Moses* (New York: HarperOne, 2003).

agree with the compositional nature of the Pentateuch but disagree with the traditional dating schemas.[6] Still others have identified additional sources such as H (a distinct voice within material often associated with P) or R (the redactor who brought various sources together into a unified form prior to the final canonical form). Third, it is far from clear what role the final compositional hand played. Was P the final redactor, such that the final form conveys a priestly bias? Was a redactor involved who imposed his or her own agenda on all the sources? If so, is this redactor the primary canonical voice? Or are we dealing with a preservationist who merely arranged the available sources chronologically to tell a coherent story, while resisting the urge (as much as possible) to assert his or her own voice?[7]

This commentary treats Genesis as a unified text without presuming to have settled the intractable issues of authorship and composition. When most relevant to interpretation, diverse source theories will be acknowledged. Even so, this brief survey of the compositional landscape gets us no closer to a single urban context for Genesis. Rather, it highlights the likelihood that the authors/redactors involved were exposed to a wide variety of ancient Near East urban contexts.

Perhaps a better way to approach the relationship of Genesis to cities is to survey what the text itself says about them. Though we later discuss these texts in greater detail, it is illuminating to sample several of them in advance to gain a sense of the book's urban ethos. Toward that end we have analyzed each time the primary Hebrew word for city

---

[5] *E.g.*, Paul J. Kissling, *Genesis*, The College Press NIV Commentary, vol. 1 (Joplin, MO: College Press, 2004), 42-51.

[6] *E.g.*, Victor P. Hamilton, *The Book of Genesis: Chapters 1-17*, The New International Commentary on the Old Testament (Grand Rapids: Eerdmans, 1990), 11-38.

[7] *Cf.* Baden, *Composition of the Pentateuch*, 248.

(*'iyr*) occurs and have taken note of the text's overall urban sensibility. That these passages span various sources suggests either that the various authorial voices are somewhat unified on this topic or that a final redactor has imposed such unity upon them. This unity would not be compromised but confirmed if one were to do a more comprehensive survey of Genesis' portrayal of urban centers. We have organized our findings under nine categories:

1. The first city was built by Cain and is a place of alienation and murder (ch 4).
2. The next major city, Babel, showcases the power and hubris of urban centers (ch 11, cf. 10:12).
3. Abraham's nephew Lot moves to the cities of Sodom and Gomorrah, which are presented as the epitome of moral degradation and uniquely worthy of swift divine intervention (chs. 18–19; cf. 13:12).
4. Abraham later encounters a Hittite city that takes advantage of him while he is trying to secure a burial plot for his family (ch 23).
5. Haran serves throughout Genesis as a city where the patriarchs are tempted to settle down rather than strive towards the fulfillment of God's promises (chs. 24, 29–31; cf. 11:31).
6. Jacob and his children find Shechem to be a city of rape and make it into a city of deceptive alliances and violent revenge (ch 34; cf. 33:18).
7. In Esau's lineage, cities are presented as power centers built by foreign kings (ch 36).
8. Though the word for city is not used, no survey of Genesis would be complete without acknowledging the central role of Egypt's capital in Genesis 37–50. Joseph first encounters this city as a site of slave trafficking (37:28, 36).
9. When a famine strikes all the surrounding lands, Egyptian cities become storehouses of food, which

>Egypt's kings use to economically exploit and eventually enslave its vulnerable neighbors (41:48; 47:21), including the Israelites (Exod 1).[8]

If all we knew about cities in Genesis were the bleak picture painted above, then we might wonder whether it is even worth engaging Genesis from an urban missiological perspective. Genesis has so little positive to say that it may be tempting to shake the dust off our feet and pursue rural mission instead. Yet these stories of urban misadventure are punctuated with vignettes of God's grace.

Even though Cain was banished from the soil and chose to make an urban living for himself, God's protective mark went with Cain and served as a reminder of divine grace (ch 4). Even though the building of Babel served as an affront to divine authority, God graciously intervened by confusing human language and keeping its inhabitants from heading down a path that would only lead to destruction (ch 11). Even though Sodom had become morally bankrupt, God was willing to spare the city on account of Abraham if a righteous contingent were found in it (ch 18). Even though God planned to overthrow Sodom and the surrounding cities, he spared Zoar at Lot's request (ch 19). Even though cities were fraught with conflict, Beersheba was remembered for conflict resolution (ch 26). Even though Jacob haggles with God in the city of Bethel, it nonetheless becomes a reminder of God's promises and protection (ch 28). Even though Haran tempted God's people away from their mission, this city provided three matriarchs who preserved Abraham's bloodline (chs. 24 and 29).

Cities can certainly be godless places when it comes to human behavior, but they are also hope-filled places where God's presence can be seen, and grace can be poured out.

---

[8] God uses the Egyptians to save many lives, including Jacob's house. Yet this does not negate the fact that Egyptian rulers abused their power on loan from God and eventually dominated over those whom they once blessed.

Structure of Genesis

Despite competing theories regarding the composition of Genesis, scholars tend to agree that any attempt to determine the structure of Genesis should begin with the *toledoth* formula. Ten times in Genesis[9] a particular subsection begins with a two-word phrase that is translated a few different ways in the NRSV: "these are the generations of" (2:4), "these are the descendants of" (6:9; 10:1; 11:10; 11:27; 25:12; 25:19; 36:1; and 36:9), "this is a list of the descendants of" (5:1),[10] and "this is the story of the family of" (37:2). The presence of this *toledoth* formula throughout Genesis and its complete absence in other books of the Pentateuch[11] suggest that the author or an editor has offered a deliberate clue as to the book's basic structure.

1. "These are the generations of the heavens and the earth" introduces a narrative that includes the creation of humans in Eden, the expulsion of humans from the garden, Cain's murder of Abel, Cain's urban legacy, and the beginning of Seth's lineage (2:4).

2. "These are the generations of Adam"[12] introduces a genealogy of Adam's descendants through Seth's

---

[9] Eleven if you separate the two concerning Esau in 36:1 and 9.

[10] The Hebrew of this passage differs slightly from the rest because the demonstrative pronoun is singular ("this" instead of "these") and because the word *safer*, translated "list," is placed between the demonstrative pronoun and the term *toledoth*.

[11] Though the full formula is not used elsewhere, the root term is used three times in Exodus (6:16, 19; 28:10) and several times in Numbers (ch. 1 and 3:1) to introduce descendants of Israel's various tribes. In neither book is it used to introduce narratives.

[12] The NRSV translation masks the fact that the *toledoth* formula in this verse differs slightly from all the others and literally reads, "*This is the book of* the genealogy of." Richard Elliot Freedman suggests that ch. 5 was a separate document and that its lead sentence became the basis of the formulaic framework that a later redactor used to weave

lineage, which culminates in the sons of Noah and is followed by a brief narrative about the sons of God who wreak havoc on the earth (5:1).

3. "These are the generations of Noah" introduces a narrative that includes the flood and its aftermath and culminates in the cursing of Ham, blessing of Shem, and death of Noah (6:9).

4. "These are the generations of the sons of Noah" introduces a genealogy of Noah's sons that culminates in the line of Shem, from whom Abraham descends, and a narrative of the city of Babel (10:1).

5. "These are the generations of Shem" introduces a genealogy of Shem's descendants that culminates in Terah and his three sons, one of whom is Abraham (11:10).

6. "These are the generations of Terah" introduces a lengthy narrative that comprises the entire life of Abraham and culminates in his death (11:27).

7. "These are the generations of Ishmael" introduces a brief genealogy that names the twelve sons of Ishmael, Abraham's firstborn son, and identifies the territories where they settled (25:12).

8. "These are the generations of Isaac" introduces a lengthy narrative that focuses on the lives of Esau and Jacob and ends in Isaac's death (25:19).

9. "These are the generations of Esau" introduces three genealogies of Esau's descendants—the second of which also begins with the *toledoth* formula (v. 9) and the third of which names the various clans that emerged from Esau's children (36:1).

10. "These are the generations of Jacob" introduces a lengthy narrative that centers on the life of Joseph and the eventual relocation of Jacob's family to Egypt and

---

together all the various sources of Genesis (*The Bible with Sources Revealed*, 40).

ends in the death of Jacob and the reconciliation of his estranged sons (37:2).

These brief summaries make clear that the namesake of each *toledoth* formula pertains not to the lead character of the section that follows, but to the progenitor of the major characters therein. As such, the forward-looking formulas anticipate the forward-moving narratives and genealogies that span Genesis. Though its fifty chapters typically proceed in a straightforward chronological way, the *toledoth* formula combines a series of insightful genealogies and lively narratives into an overarching story in such a way as to advance and deepen its plotline.

The structure of Genesis may also be analyzed on the basis of its parallel sections. Thomas L. Brodie has recently argued that Genesis is comprised of twenty-six pairs of corresponding accounts. He calls these "diptychs," drawing upon the image of two-paneled paintings. We have two creation accounts (1:1-2:4a // 2:4b-24), two sin accounts (2:25-3:24 // 4:1-16), two genealogies (4:17-26 // ch. 5), two halves of the flood account (chs. 6-7 // 8:1-9:17), two accounts of Noah's sons after the flood (9:18-29 // ch. 10), and so forth.[13] Brodie goes on to identify six diptychs in the primeval history, seven in Abraham's narrative, six in Jacob's narrative, and seven in Joseph's narrative. Not all paired panels are parallel in the same way. Some cover a similar topic (12:1-13:1 // 13:2-18); others relate by way of contrast (ch. 34 // 35:1-20). In some, the second panel zooms in on a dimension of the first (1:1-2:4a // 2:4b-24); in others, panel two simply complements panel one (ch. 49 // ch. 50). What results is a multifaceted approach to the various events that make up the Genesis saga. The narrative itself is a lively dialogue that beckons us into the conversation. Readers are encouraged not only to read Genesis forward, interpreting later events in light of earlier

---

[13] For a chart containing all the diptychs, see Thomas L. Brodie, *Genesis As Dialogue: A Literary, Historical, & Theological Commentary* (Oxford: Oxford University Press, 2001), 300.

ones but to read diptychs more closely, each half in light of the other, to discern what additional parallels might lay right beneath the surface.

While acknowledging the important insights of the *toledoth* and diptych approaches, for the purposes of this commentary, we follow a rather simple interpretive outline that showcases the missional importance of Genesis. While simple, this structure connects with the theological agenda of the final editor or author of Genesis. The Bible story has direction away from the mess humans make of this world, toward the new world God is making.

Creation's Collapse (Gen 1-11)   *Creation's Hope (Gen 12-50)*

- Creation (1:1-2:25)
- Fall & Aftermath (3:1-6:4)
- Flood & Aftermath (6:5-11:32)

- Abraham & Sons (12:1-25:18)
- Isaac & Sons (25:19-36:43)
- Jacob & Sons (37:1-50:26)

This structure is simple and yet descriptive enough to convey the big picture of what Genesis is about. It takes as its point of departure the commonly accepted twofold division of Genesis: prehistory (Gen 1-11) and patriarchal history (Gen 12-50). It makes explicit that Genesis 1-11 sets up the problem to which Genesis 12-50 is the solution. It also seeks to correct an all too common overemphasis on Genesis 1-3 by expanding the "Fall" account of Genesis properly to include chapters 4-11. The ills with which this world suffers are not limited to what a single couple could forfeit within the context of an ideal environment. What ails this world penetrates deeply into sibling relations, social structures, governmental authorities, parent-child dynamics, and all human attempts at civilization in the corrupt world in which we live.

The story of Abraham and his offspring is not simply the beginning of the formation of a people who will procreate long enough to eventually beget the Messiah who will save this world. Rather, the creation of a set apart people in history *is* God's primary offering of hope to the world that is fallen. It is not merely prefatory, but essential to what

God was and is doing about the serial dysfunction that permeates human and nonhuman creation as graphically portrayed in Gen 1-11.

Research Methodology

Genesis is a long and rich book. Since its first eleven chapters have seen an inordinate degree of scholarly engagement, we have divided our Genesis commentary into two parts: chapters 1-11 and chapters 12-50. This volume focuses on Genesis 1-11. In order to keep our conversations freshly attuned to twenty-first century missional concerns, this volume focuses on books and especially articles that have been written since 2000. Though this will keep our conversation fresh, it means readers will have to look elsewhere if they want more thorough and exhaustive treatment of all the issues. This does not mean that we will be setting aside all insights we have gained from twentieth-century works. We stand on their broad shoulders and owe them a debt of gratitude we will never be able to pay. Still, in a field of research that continues to grow exponentially, it is no longer possible to read and keep up to date on everything. One must be selective, and more than enough has been written since the turn of the millennium to provoke disciplined and insightful analysis of the Bible's first book.

CREATION 1:1—2:25

Seven Day Creation: Genesis 1:1—2:3

> **Cities in the Divine Plan**
>
> As modern readers of a highly urbanized world one of the thoughts or questions we have entering into the story of Genesis is whether or not cities were part of divine origin. Did God intend for cities to bloom and flourish or were they merely happenstance? The challenge then becomes how much or how little do we read what has taken place throughout urban history back into the text of Genesis.
>
> *Sean Benesh*

Genesis begins with a seven-day creation account that furnishes the foundation of our understanding of God's mission in this world. It also serves as the battleground for countless debates between believers and unbelievers, conservatives and liberals, theologians and ancient Near East historians. We will not fully enter these debates or try to answer their questions once and for all.[14] The primary question we ask is this: What did Genesis 1 reveal to God's people that they did not already know, and how does this inform our understanding of God's mission?

The ancient Israelites did not need to be told that creation came into existence through divine agency. This was commonplace among the inhabitants of the Fertile Crescent. They did not need to be informed that humans were unique among God's creatures and exercise an unparalleled measure of control over it. God's people needed no help figuring out that animals, like humans, are composed of gendered sets and that males and females must mate for their species to reproduce. They were well aware that the sun and moon provided light and were

---

[14] To learn more about such questions, see David Wilkinson, "Reading Genesis 1-3 in the Light of Modern Science," in *Reading Genesis after Darwin*, eds. Stephen C. Barton and David Wilkinson (Oxford: Oxford University Press, 2009): 127-144.

helpful for demarcating time. The original recipients of Genesis would have known all of this from experience. So, we must avoid the modern presumption that ancient folk were so dull that a prophet of God had to impart such elementary information to them.

To truly appreciate what these texts reveal, we need to exercise historical imagination. What would have stood out to the original hearers? What would have made a statement in their time and place? Such questions are not an alien scholarly imposition on the text. It is one of the basic ways we encounter the text. It provokes a response in us, as it would have in them, based on what stood out. There is no need for us to pinpoint exactly when Genesis was written to surmise an answer to such questions. It is enough to know that the ancient Israelites grew up amid the religious and political worldviews of Babylon, Assyria, Egypt, and Canaan. Most scholars agree on that much. What would have stood out in Genesis 1, then, is how its presentation of God, creation, and humanity differed from other ideas that circulated throughout the ancient world.

All too often we read Genesis in order to find divine authorization for contemporary human agendas. We want assurance that humans are the pinnacle of creation, that all creatures cower under our sway, that all celestial bodies shine primarily for us, and that God's design for wholesome society is exactly what we have discovered it to be. We assume that ancient society was as ego-centric as we are. Even if it were, the biblical author need not have been massaging ancient egos. Given the thrust of Genesis 1-11—where desire for autonomy is the root of all sin and confidence in human potential leads to a civil engineering project that God sees fit to disrupt—it is more likely that the author implored readers to take their eyes off themselves and direct them toward the creator. They needed no help seeing things from a human perspective. Like us, they needed to embrace a God's eye view of creation.

1:1-2 In the Beginning

> **Urban Planning and the *Imago Dei***
>
> We will soon discover that humanity is made in the image of God. What we find from the very beginning is God is creative and a creator. Regardless of what we interpret *Imago Dei* to mean all we need to do is look around and we will see this latent creativity exploding out of humanity. This goes beyond the arts but is evident in everything we do and we're about. In regard to cities we note creativity from architecture to urban planning to transportation to new construction standards to mixed-use developments and so much more. It doesn't mean we haven't created unhealthy cities as well through our creativity. But we learn, move forward, adapt and retrofit.
>
> *Sean Benesh*

The first word of Genesis has sparked considerable debate among Bible scholars.[15] The point of contention is whether this word (*bereshith*) should be translated in an absolute or construct sense, both of which are legitimate renderings of the Hebrew. In other words, should the initial clause be translated "In the beginning, God created the heavens and the earth" or "When God began to create the heavens and the earth"? At stake is whether or not the Genesis author credited God for fashioning everything from nothing (*ex nihilo*) or whether matter preexisted alongside God and

---

[15] David Tuesday Adamo, "The Genesis Creation Accounts: An African Background," in *Genesis*. Texts @ Contexts Series (Minneapolis: Fortress, 2010), 25-33; James E. Atwell, "An Egyptian Source for Genesis 1," *Journal of Theological Studies* 51, pt. 2 (Oct 2000): 441-477; Gordon H. Johnston, "Genesis 1 and Ancient Egyptian Creation Myths," *Bibliotheca Sacra* 165 (Apr-Jun 2008): 178-94; Johnson Teng Kok Lim, "Explication of an Exegetical Enigma in Genesis 1:1-3," *The Asia Journal of Theology* 16, no. 2 (Oct 2002): 301-314; and "Genesis 1-11 and its Ancient Near Eastern Parallels," *The Asia Journal of Theology* 19, vol. 1 (Apr 2005): 68-78; and Jiří Moskala, "Interpretation of $b^e re'\check{s}\hat{\imath}t$ in the Context of Genesis 1:1-3," *Andrews University Seminary Studies* 49, no. 1 (Spring 2011): 33-44.

simply needed to be subdued or appropriated for God's creative purposes.

This debate carries into verse 2. Is the depiction of the heavens and earth as "a formless void" the end result of God's having initially created matter *or* the condition of matter before God began to mold it? This question becomes more pressing for those who depict Genesis 1 as a combat myth between Israel's God and the gods of other nations. In the ancient Near East, it is certainly possible for a "formless void" to denote a chaotic pool of warring deities that must be vanquished in order to create habitable space for God's creatures. Ancient Sumerian creation accounts like *Enuma Elish* begin with chaos, and ancient Canaanites associated storms and seas with deities. Moreover, other Old Testament passages freely appropriate mythological language and link it to the legacy of Israel's God (e.g., Job 26:12; Ps 74:14; 89:10; and Isa 51:9).

As plausible as such a depiction may have been in its context, several scholars have rejected it, and with good reason.[16] Were verse 2 introducing a combat myth, we would expect a conflictual account to follow. Instead, we find a quite peaceful and orderly endeavor. So orderly, in fact, that it is more fitting to translate "a formless void" (*tohu wavohu*) as "unformed and unfilled."[17] For the creation account is a symmetrical poem that entails three days of *forming* and three days of *filling*.

---

[16] See Catherine Keller, "'Be This Fish': A Theology of Creation out of Chaos," *Word & World* 32, no. 1 (Winter 2012): 15-20; John H. Walton, "Creation in Genesis 1:1-2:3 and the Ancient Near East: Order out of Disorder after *Chaoskampt*," *Calvin Theological Journal* 43 (2008): 48-63.

[17] See Kissling, *Genesis*, vol. 1, 93-95.

	Forming		Filling
Day 1	Light & Dark	**Day 4**	Sun, Moon, & Stars Day & Night
Day 2	Sky & waters	**Day 5**	Birds & fish
Day 3	Dry land	**Day 6**	Land Creatures & Humans

The "unformed" condition described in v. 2 corresponds to the first three days of creation, and the "unfilled" condition corresponds to the next three days. Moreover, there is no evidence that God faces resistance or hostility on any of these days. God forms and fills at will, and all of creation yields to the creative divine word.

Even without the combat motif, it is not clear that Genesis 1:1 emphasizes creation *ex nihilo*. The Hebrew Scriptures seem uninterested in philosophical questions about the preexistence of matter. It was not a debate for them—not something that needed to be emphasized or proven.[18] It was more important to the ancient Israelites that their God created this world without opposition and that the world they inhabited was orderly and good. Whether before or after the initial act of creation, the earth was formless and empty as God began the weeklong creation project.

1:3—2:1 Six Days

A key issue surrounding the interpretation of the seven-day creation account is its purpose. Does this chapter exist to demonstrate God's triumph over the primordial gods that once held sway over the cosmos, as many who have brought it into conversation with ancient Near Eastern mythologies have argued? Or, does it exist to explain the

---

[18] It later became important to God's people around the first century BCE. The author of 2 Maccabees goes out of his way to make it clear, saying, "look at the heaven and the earth and see everything that is in them, and recognize that God did not make them out of things that existed. And in the same way the human race came into being" (7:28).

material origins of the universe, as many who have brought it into conversation with modern science have argued? Evangelical scholar John Walton rejects these two positions and argues, instead, that it is an anthropic or human-centered account that establishes the function and functionaries of the cosmos on behalf of humankind.[19]

Function for Humans

According to Walton, the creation of light and dark, day and night, on day one marks the creation of time. The formation of the sky on day two signals the creation of weather. The appearance of dry land and vegetation on day three provides the means of agriculture and human sustenance. The respective functionaries of these domains are installed on days four through six. Regardless of when the sun and moon first existed materially, a description of their function for humans is supplied on day four. Aquatic and aerial functionaries are identified on day five, and land animals, including humans, on day six.

The linchpin for Walton's functional schema is day seven. Having established that cosmos and temple are nearly synonymous in the ancient worldview, he observes that the gods of the ancient world routinely rested in their holy temples after having subdued the cosmos. With all things in order, they manage ongoing affairs from there.[20] Walton sees something like this happening in Genesis—only, Israel's God is the one who ordered the cosmos, ascribed functions to its occupants, and took residence in his holy temple in order to run things from there.

Another approach to the purpose of Genesis 1 focuses on polemics. That is, the seven-day creation account serves to replace superstitious polytheistic accounts with a sanitized,

---

[19] Walton, "Creation in Genesis 1:1-2:3 and the Ancient Near East"; and *The Lost World of Genesis One: Ancient Cosmology and the Origins Debate* (Downers Grove, IL: InterVarsity Press, 2009).

[20] Walton, "Creation in Genesis 1:1-2:3," 61.

demythologized Israelite one. It shows how all things came into existence through Israel's God and that all created things lack divine status. The sun, moon, stars, storms, seas, and sea monsters are merely products of divine creativity.

These various approaches are not mutually exclusive. Nearly all of them are compatible with the polemical approach, and it would be easy to merge a functional approach with one emphasizing the material origins of the universe (though Walton does not). Still, neither of them convincingly identifies the precise purpose that this account would have served for its original audience. Though Genesis 1 offers a clear alternative to ancient mythology, its polemical nature is not the thrust as much as the means. It does not offer the *why* as much as the *how*. The question remains, *what* was the author seeking to communicate in polemical fashion?

Though Walton's critique of materialistic and divine conflict motives seems right, certain aspects of his approach do not satisfy. Whereas a case can be made that days 1-3 establish the conditions necessary for human survival, we are nowhere informed of the function of stars, birds, sea creatures, and land animals on days 4-6. The greater and lesser lights function for humans insofar as they help us keep time, but the stars and other creatures are presented as if for their own sake. Moreover, the sky, waters, land, and vegetation function on behalf of nonhuman creatures as much as, if not more than, for humans. This leads to a related shortcoming. If not everything in this account fulfills a purpose that serves humans, Walton's human-centered perspective is suspect. In a world where humans eat of plants and trees only (v. 29),[21] most living creatures contribute little to humans, except perhaps responsibility, to the extent that humans are required to exercise dominion over them. But what

---

[21] Humans are not authorized to eat animal flesh until after the flood (Gen 9:3).

does it look like for humans to exercise dominion over the sea monsters? What function could such creatures possibly have served for ancient Israelites whose aquatic vessels could hardly navigate the depths of the Mediterranean Sea? In Job 41, God makes clear that humans are powerless before Leviathan, which is likely one of the sea monsters referred to in Genesis 1:21. There are also problems with Walton's depiction of day seven, but those will be discussed in our treatment of 2:2-3.

A Place for Everything

> ### Order and Place
>
> God's creation entails order, as we will see, both spatially and relationally. That alone is a key insight into the health or unhealth of cities ... when things are ***out*** of order. This, too, is both seen and experienced spatially and relationally. We see this spatially when negligent urban planning plots our cities on a course that leads to unhealth whether through car-dependent sprawl, lack of access to jobs and services for low-income families, or policies and zoning that favor the wealthy. We also see disorder played out too often through race riots because of the mistreatment of minorities, political protests in light of unsavory policies, and the like. Why do these things happen? There is disorder which plays out spatially and relationally.
>
> *Sean Benesh*

How then should we understand the purpose of the seven-day creation account? A better way emphasizes not conflict, material origins, or function—but place, conceived both spatially and relationally. Spatially speaking, it is quite clear that the created entities of days 4-6 occupy the space God fashioned on days 1-3. Though this would not have revealed anything new to the original hearers, how the author communicates it conveys much.

One could easily reflect on the wide array of creatures and celestial bodies that inhabit the cosmos and observe how chaotic and even violent it all seems. Humans kill humans who kill animals, which in turn kill other animals and occasionally humans. Birds and bears frequently pounce on the waters to snatch fish, if they are not themselves picked off by some other animal. Swarms of locusts inundate fields and ravage crops that already have difficulty surviving droughts and heat waves. Other insects invade human dwellings uninvited, bringing discomfort and disease to their inhabitants. This is why ancient Mesopotamians often narrated creation and crop cycles in terms of chaos and conflict: they were projecting their own turbulent life experiences in mythological terms.

It was therefore an act of faith that a Hebrew poet would cast a contrary vision of order and complementarity. The disarray of human experience hangs on the scaffolding of divine order and intentionality. There is a time and a place for everything, and those with eyes to see will perceive all things in their place. Genesis 1 may have something to do with material origins, function, and polemic, but the emphasis is *order*—an order that is all too easy for technologically advanced societies to take for granted.

God's good order was not limited to space. Our account also depicts creation as a sort of relational hierarchy. Though stars, birds, fish, and animals exist as good creatures in and of themselves, they stand in a specific sort of relationship to humans. God supplies plants as food for humans and animals. The sun and moon rule over day and night. *All* humans bear God's image and exercise dominion over living and breathing creatures.

This hierarchy would have been quite revelatory at the time it was written. It stands in contrast to the *Enuma Elish*, for instance, in which humans were created as slaves to provide food for various gods by butchering and burning animals. It rejects Egyptian religion in which the sun was a god and only Pharaoh bore the divine image and could exercise dominion. It denies Assyrian astrology in which stars were deities that dictated the direction of human history. It spurns Canaanite mythology in which sea monsters (among other created beings) were also gods to be feared and placated. Finally, it stands out among nearly all ancient cultures in failing to clearly situate females beneath males, commoners beneath royalty, and slaves beneath free persons in the relational hierarchy.

God's Image

> **Notion of a Just City**
>
> In this section we begin to see the notion of a just city. If we're to exercise influence on behalf of God what should that look like for our cities? How do we faithfully represent God in positions or influences of authority loaned to us to manage, sustain, and care for our cities?
>
> *Sean Benesh*

There is little consensus as to what it means that humans were created in God's image.[22] Walton rightly notes that, after building temples, ancient folk placed images of their gods in them.[23] Though it is far from clear that Genesis 1 depicts God as building a temple and personally entering it, on day six God clearly installs humans amid creation to bear the divine image. This, too, may be a polemic against ancient polytheism. The Israelites must not build images of God and place them anywhere since humans are the only acceptable divine image in God's good creation (Exod 20:4).

This has been interpreted as conveying privilege upon humans—the right to rule as they see fit. Given the context of Genesis, which denies humans absolute power (Gen 2:16-17), it is more likely that such language conveyed both freedom and limitation. Humans were *free* from the antiquated notion that imperial rulers, mysterious creatures, celestial bodies, or powerful forces were divine. There are no divine or quasi-divine intermediaries between

---

[22] For superb analysis, see J. Richard Middleton's *The Liberating Image: The Imago Dei in Genesis One* (Grand Rapids: Brazos Press, 2005).

[23] Walton, "Creation in Genesis 1:1-2:3," 60-61.

humans and God—no one else to fear and to serve.[24] Humans were also *limited* in their dominion. Their special status in creation is derivative. They exercise influence on behalf of God, who stands above them and who will call them to account if they fail to faithfully represent their creator or if they abuse the authority they have on loan from him.

Genesis 1 does not tell us exactly what human rule as God's image entails. Bible readers often place an unbearable burden on Genesis 1 by asking it to explain more than it actually does. Yet this chapter does not cast a comprehensive vision for human existence or the mission of God's people. Instead, it sets forth a very basic framework for locating the *place* of all things in God's creation. Loaded terms like "our image" and "dominion" are not final answers as much as conceptual placeholders.[25] We must continue reading the story of this God to find out who the "our" of "our image" is, what that image conveys, and what dominion truly means.

Genesis 1 sets limits, raises questions, and points readers forward to a story that is only beginning to unfold. Expecting this chapter to do more than this often means co-opting its words to deliver our own message. This practice has emboldened countless humans to exploit God's good creation in the name of dominion. The common corrective is to insist that dominion here means something else. A more fundamental corrective is to recognize the placeholding nature of such language and encourage readers to look forward in the story for further clues as its meaning.

---

[24] Angels are not introduced in Genesis 1. They may be implied in the phrase "let us make humankind in our image" (v. 26). We will return to this possibility in connection with 3:22.

[25] See Richard S. Briggs, "Humans in the Image of God and Other Things Genesis Does Not Make Clear," *Journal of Theological Interpretation* 4.1 (2010): 111-126.

2:2-3 Day Seven

The clearest example of a placeholder in the first creation account happens on day seven. Because God finished working and rested on this day, it is holy or set apart. Though readers are told which day is set apart, we are not told for what purpose day seven is set apart. One must keep reading and then draw meaning from the story as it unfolds. This is one place in early Genesis where scholars have reached a strong consensus. God sets day seven apart in anticipation of the Torah's commands that the Israelites must rest on the seventh day (Exod 20:11). As God rested on day seven, so the Israelites must rest.

This command had important social and economic implications for Israel. The wealthy had always enjoyed regular times of rest, but the poor, the enslaved, the animals, and the land seldom did. Since creation was meant to be enjoyed by all creatures, God filled Israel's calendar with days, weeks, and even years of rest for all creation (Lev 25). Creation is, above all, God's gift. Though work will have its place in creation, work is not an end in itself. As Jesus later clarified, humans were not made for Sabbath, but Sabbath for humans (Mark 2:27) so we may enjoy the beauty and wholeness of God's good creation.

A Day of Rest in the City

If we are to set aside and rest one day a week "so we may enjoy the beauty and wholeness of God's good creation" then how is that played out in cities. For many, rest or times of spiritual refreshment only happen **away** from the city. It is assumed that the only way to truly rest or connect deeply with God is outside of the city in the wilderness. But what would it look like to do this in the city? Even more so, if God truly designed us and called us to take a day to rest and reflect, then how crucial is this for cities to have adequate parks and green spaces? Too often the poor reside in parts of the city with few opportunities for outdoor recreation in the city and certainly don't have the means or access to leave the city to recreate in wilderness areas. How should this then motivate us about making our

> cities healthier (physically and spatially) so that regardless of one's socio-economic standing there are ample green spaces to rest in and enjoy.
>
> *Sean Benesh*

For Walton, this interpretation does not exhaust the meaning of Genesis 2:2-3. After convincingly arguing that Genesis does not depict creation in conflictual terms borrowed from ancient Near Eastern mythology, he uses those same myths to frame his understanding of divine rest on day seven. Having established functional order, Walton goes onto argue that Israel's God follows the gods of mythology by resting in the newly minted cosmic sanctuary and exercising control from there. Yet there is no clear evidence on day seven—or any other day—that God settled or rested *amid creation*. It is not enough to observe that the ancients said such things about their gods; the book of Genesis lacks this motif altogether. God never takes residence on earth or even among the celestial bodies named on day four. It is more accurate to say that God created humans in his image so we may serve as a proxy for his presence amid creation.

Genesis presumes that after fashioning the heavens and earth the creator remained in the heavenly abode from which he called forth all creation. This super-celestial dwelling is presumed in the flood account when God destroys the earth without having first to depart from it. It is presumed in the Babel account when God has to "come down" to see the humans' impressive city project with its prominent tower reaching into the "heavens" (11:5). It is clear in Jacob's vision of God that entails a ladder spanning heaven and earth with angels ascending and descending upon it (28:12).

Nor will it do to assert that God dwelled among creation in the garden of Eden only before humans sinned and then, as a result, he chose or was compelled to leave. There is no evidence that God dwelled among humans before the Fall in a manner significantly different from after the Fall. Though readers routinely presume divine and human cohabitation and social interaction in Eden, Genesis 2-3 is remarkably silent about such matters. After creating and placing humans in the garden, God shows up initially to impart instructions and later to impart judgment. God does not go on periodic walks *with humans*, nor did they participate together in some form of recreation. What little divine-human interaction is recorded prior to the Fall continues unabated after the Fall. This is evident in God's familial conversations with Cain in 4:6-7 and with Abraham in chapter 18. One might protest that greater intimacy is presupposed before the Fall because God reached down to form Adam from dirt. Yet immediately after the Fall, God also, quite intimately, helped Eve with her first child (4:1). Moreover, the text is quite clear that the Fall resulted in *humans* being kicked out of Eden, not *God*. Indeed, it is only by reading divine residency into Genesis 2-3 in the first place that one is able to lament its absence.[26]

The emphasis of day seven is not divine habitation, but the cessation of a specific form of divine activity. Three times in Genesis 2:2-3 the author emphasizes that God ceased or rested *from work* on day seven. Not once does it indicate *where* God rested. Divine rest may well signal creation's readiness to function according to God's design, but supposing human and divine cohabitation this early in the biblical narrative has significant repercussions for the overall shape of the biblical narrative and the place of God's mission within it. Though Walton does not argue this, it is quite common for readers to narrate the Bible story in terms of spatial union with God in Eden, followed by spatial separation such that God retreats to heaven, followed by Jesus who bridged the gap between heaven and earth, which makes possible a spatial reunion between humans and God *in heaven*. The church's mission then becomes one of announcing this separation and its resolution in Christ. It frames Christian hope in terms of

---

[26] See commentary below on Genesis 3 for more on this theme.

vacating this earth for a future heavenly abode. Yet as we continue through Genesis we see that this is neither the shape of the Bible story nor the focus of Christian mission.

Creation of Humans and Animals: Genesis 2:4-25

2:4-17 The Garden and the Human

The second creation account begins much like the first one. It, too, describes an initial state of creation that wasn't quite complete. There were no plants, herbs, or fields upon the earth because there were no rains to irrigate them and no humans to work the ground (v. 5). God then provides the water and humans necessary to carry forward his creative purposes (vv. 6-7).[27]

These verses raise so many interesting questions that it is often difficult to discern what issues were most important to the author. When did these things happen? Where exactly was this garden? Why doesn't the order of creation in this chapter mesh neatly with chapter 1? Since standard commentaries routinely address these perennial questions, I focus on recent theories impacting the interpretation of Genesis 2, especially as they shed light on our understanding of Christian mission.

---

[27] Though most translations give the impression that the earth was well watered at this time by a stream or mist, Max Rogland suggests that v. 6 depicts God as furnishing a rain-producing cloud that he intended to meet the needs of forthcoming vegetation. God first provides the rain cloud and then he provides the human. See "Interpreting אד in Genesis 2.5-6: Neglected Rabbinic and Intertextual Evidence," in *Journal for the Study of the Old Testament* 34, no. 4 (2010): 379-93. Though the grammar of 2:6 is not clear on this account (e.g., there is no *vav*-consecutive appended to the verb), the key term, which the NRSV translates as "stream," could mean "rain producing cloud" (as in Jer 10:13 and Ps 135:7). This makes better sense of the claim in v. 5 that there hasn't been enough water to provide for plants. If there was an adequate water supply all along in the form of a stream or mist, then why is the absence of rain a contributing factor worth mentioning in v. 5?

Garden Temple?

Lately, scholars have been making much of parallels between the garden of Eden and the tabernacle or Jerusalem temple.[28] These parallels sometimes inform their understanding of Christian mission. G. K. Beale has been most influential in this regard. His thesis about God's tabernacling presence in the garden establishes a strong link between Adam's purpose, Israel's vocation, and the church's mission:

> Adam's purpose in that first garden-temple was to expand its boundaries until it circumscribed the earth, so that the earth would be completely filled with God's glorious presence. Adam's failure led, in time, to the re-establishment of the tabernacle and temple in Israel. Both were patterned after the model of Eden and were constructed to symbolize the entire cosmos in order to signify that Israel's purpose as corporate Adam was to extend its borders by faithfully obeying God and spreading his glorious presence throughout the earth. . . . *The church is to be God's temple, so filled with his glorious presence that we expand and fill the earth with that presence until God finally accomplishes the goal completely at the end of time!* This is our common mission. May the church of the twenty-first century unite in order to attain this goal (emphasis original).[29]

---

[28] See G. K. Beale, *The Temple and the Church's Mission: A Biblical Theology of the Dwelling Place of God*, New Studies in Biblical Theology 17 (Downers Grove, IL: Intervarsity Press, 2004), 66-80; Robert M. Hinckly Jr., "Adam, Aaron, and the Garden Sanctuary," *Logia* 4 (2013): 5-12; Lifsa Block Schachter, "The Garden of Eden as God's First Sanctuary," *Jewish Bible Quarterly* 41, no. 2 (Apr-Jun 2013): 73-77; and Walton, *The Lost World of Genesis One*, 82-83.

[29] Beale, *The Temple and the Church's Mission*, 369 . . . 402. See also, Christopher J. H. Wright, *The Mission of God: Unlocking the Bible's Grand Narrative* (Downers Grove, IL: InterVarsity, 2006), 334-40.

If Beale is right, then recovering the sense of divine presence once enjoyed in Eden is central to Christian mission. Consider his evidence. Beale enumerates eleven parallels between the garden of Eden and Israel's sanctuaries.[30] The sheer number of parallels appears to be quite compelling—but a number of weak points do not add up to a strong point. At the risk of overkill, I briefly present and critique each of Beale's alleged parallels.

1. The garden, like the tabernacle, is the unique place of God's presence since he walked and talked with Adam there.

   Yet, importantly, Genesis never says that God uniquely resided in the garden. Furthermore, God never walks *with Adam* (see commentary on 3:8), and he continues talking with people after the Fall without any apparent interruption.

2. The garden housed the first priest. Though Adam is never identified by overt priestly language, he is called to "serve" and "keep" the garden. In Torah, priests are said to "serve" in the tabernacle and they are repeatedly called to "keep" Torah. Sometimes they are even called to "keep" the "service" of the tabernacle (e.g., Num 3:7-8).

   Yet these terms are quite generic and may be used with regard to a wide variety of occupations, including horticulture. They are not technical priestly terms and there is nothing priestly about Adam's status or role in these chapters. Adam represents everyone, not priestly men.

---

[30] He also supports his case with ancient Near Eastern parallels and by noting how Ezekiel and two Second Temple Jewish texts speak of Eden. I address the Ezekiel point under point 8 below. The Second Temple references say more about second century Judaism than they do Genesis 2-3, though not all of Beale's prooftexts even apply.

3. The garden is the first place we encounter cherubim, which play an important role in tabernacle and temple décor (e.g., Exod 25:18-20).

   Yet cherubim are nowhere described as being *in* the garden of Eden. They only show up *after* the Fall and they are placed *outside* the entrance to the garden to keep humans out.

4. The tree of life resembles the lampstand that we find in the tabernacle. It branches out like a tree and contains flower-like cups and petals.

   Though the lampstand is patterned after *a* tree with flowers and petals (Exod 25:31-36), there is nothing that connects it to *the* tree of life, in particular, except that the latter is a tree.

5. The temple was decorated using floral arrangements (1 Kgs 6-7), thereby drawing upon garden of Eden imagery.

   Yet there is nothing specifically Eden-like about floral arrangements. Flowers aren't even mentioned in the Eden account. The fact that floral imagery is present in temple designs and not tabernacle designs may suggest that the imagery is borrowed from royal gardens and not the Eden account.

6. Eden has a river flowing from it, just like the temple in Ezekiel 47 and God's throne in Revelation 7.

   Yet the river begins in the region of Eden, not the garden (v. 10).[31] It waters the garden before splitting off. If the garden is meant to signify God's most holy presence, this account is the only one that does not depict the river as flowing from God's most holy locale.

---

[31] Verse 8 specifies that the garden was a specific place that God planted in the wider region of Eden, so the two places are not identical but overlapping.

7. The garden is a place of two precious stones that are used in relation to the tabernacle and temple: gold and onyx.

   This evidence is doubly weak. First, Genesis 2 actually mentions three stones: gold, bdellium, and onyx. Whereas gold is widely used throughout the tabernacle and temple, bdellium is not used at all, and onyx doesn't appear in the tabernacle, but in the priestly vestment (Exod 25:7). Gold and onyx only appear together in one passage regarding the temple, and they are two of ten different precious stones (1 Chron 29:2). In other words, the three precious stones associated with Eden are never overtly grouped together in later sanctuary references. Second, and more problematic for Beale's thesis, these precious stones aren't even located in the garden of Eden. They are placed in the land of Havilah—a land that the river passes through only after it leaves the garden (Gen 2:10-12).

8. The garden is located on a mountain, just like the temple later is.

   Yet mountain language is not used of the garden of Eden in Genesis, only in Ezekiel. At most, this furnishes evidence of a connection between Ezekiel's Eden metaphor and the temple. It should not be forgotten, however, that Ezekiel's Eden is the metaphorical abode of the king of Tyre. It does not represent God's tabernacling presence, but bountiful wealth that a pagan king is about to lose.

9. The garden has a tree of wisdom and the tabernacle has the ark, which contains the Ten Commandments, which are Israel's source of wisdom.

   Yet the tree of knowledge of good and evil is more like a tree of death in contrast to the tree of life. In the wisdom literature, wisdom is not associated with the tree of knowledge, but with the tree of life (Prov 3:18). Furthermore, God's people are commanded to partake of Torah, whereas Adam was forbidden from partaking of the tree of knowledge.

10. The garden has an eastern entrance (Gen 3:24), just like the temple (Ezek 40:6).

    Yet in Genesis, the "east" serves as more of an exit than an entrance. God drives the humans out and blocks their way back in with cherubim and flaming sword to make sure that it never actually serves as an entrance. Furthermore, in the wider context of Genesis, "east" may be a symbol of trouble. Cain builds his city east of Eden and the builders of Babel also move east.[32]

11. The garden has a 3-part structure (garden, Eden, wider creation) just like the temple (most holy place, holy place, outer courtyard).

    Yet the characteristics of the three parts implied in Genesis 2-3 don't parallel the tabernacle closely enough to constitute an intertextual echo.

In sum, the equation of Eden with a divine sanctuary does not fare well under scrutiny. It turns out to be a flimsy case of "parallelomania." Though God's presence is no doubt important throughout Scripture, it is not a major theme of Genesis 2. What is more, nowhere in Genesis does God grant his people responsibility for managing, promoting, or otherwise extending the reach of his palpable presence. Those wishing to make such activities central to Christian mission should look elsewhere for support. God manifests himself at numerous points throughout the Genesis narrative, but he does so at his own discretion and without human assistance of any kind.

A Balanced Ecosystem

If divine presence in the garden is not what this account is about, what clues does the text provide as to its meaning? A first clue is how the author sets up the creation of humans. The emphasis is on creation's incompleteness. The ground could not produce vegetation without God

---

[32] Kissling, *Genesis*, vol. 1, 158.

providing sustaining rainfall and without humans providing hands to work the soil. From the start, Genesis 2 appears to be about the interconnectedness between God, humans, and land.

Such interconnectedness continues in v. 7 with the formation of the first human from the dust of the ground and the breath of life from God. Humans would not be human without God and soil. Likewise, the soil could not serve its intended purposes without God and humans. What remains is for these interdependent creations to be brought together. So God plants a garden in Eden. He puts the human in the garden and he causes every kind of tree to grow from the ground. It may seem like mere name-dropping to identify the tree of life and the tree of knowledge at this point (v. 9), but we see in verses 15-17 that it is quite significant.

Urban Ecosystem

While we're still in the pre-urban storyline of Genesis this notion of a balanced ecosystem is also an urban issue, meaning the health and wellness of city dwellers rises and falls on the health and vitality of the city related to the natural environment. Healthy cities incorporate green spaces for people to enjoy. There are psychological ramifications to this as well. Cities with ample green spaces, proper sanitation, and other open spaces are healthier than cities lacking these green spaces. Many cities have large sections who are under clouds of pollution or enveloped in the stench of open sewers. A balanced ecosystem is an urban issue.

Sean Benesh

Before focusing on humanity, the author describes a river that flows from Eden, passes through the garden, and splits off into four distinct rivers (vv. 10-14). The first river, the otherwise unknown Pishon, flows through the equally unfamiliar region of Havilah, which is rich in gold and precious stones. A second unknown river flows through the familiar land of Cush, often identified with Ethiopia. Yet Ethiopia as we know it doesn't have such a prominent river. The remaining rivers and regions are familiar: the Tigris flows east of Assyria and the Euphrates flows west of it.

The unfamiliar territory demarcated by these rivers suggests that God provides sustenance for all the lands of the world: far and near, familiar and foreign. Wherever humans end up, they inhabit land that is fertilized by the creator himself. The interconnectedness of God, humans, and soil is not simply a unique feature of Eden; it is a global phenomenon.

Limits to Human Dominion

> **Urban Freedom**
>
> Cities are ground zero for where human freedom is displayed, both for the betterment of its citizens and for their demise. Even housed within the same cities we can find freedom leading to wholeness and life and at the same time freedom leading to oppression amidst corruption. For the global poor while there is freedom to migrate to urban centers there is not the same freedom to break free from crushing poverty.
>
> *Sean Benesh*

I stated above that it is significant that the tree of life and the tree of knowledge are named among all other trees that God creates from the ground. It is significant because they are part of what God calls humans to serve and to keep (v. 15). They are not otherworldly artifacts, descending from heaven and thus demanding special reverence. They are part of the good creation over which God gave humans dominion.

This places God's command in verse 16 in a different light. Humans may eat freely from all the trees of the garden—except for the tree of knowledge of good and evil. This prohibition has sparked all sorts of speculation. Does this tree represent sexual knowledge, comprehensive knowledge, ethical knowledge? Is God trying to keep humans ignorant and therefore innocent? Is he trying to restrict freedom or does the presence of genuine choice actually validate freedom? What does it mean that they will die on the day of which they partake of the fruit? Is this a literal death or a spiritual death? A literal day or a figurative day?

The questions are legion, as are the possible answers. I focus on one that is often neglected. The fact that God's prohibition revolves around part of the created order that God placed under human jurisdiction is fitting. It is fitting because humans often stray from God's will in areas over which we've been given some sort of control. Much sin in our lives and throughout Genesis comes from thinking we can do whatever we want with the power we have been given and the people over whom we've been given responsibility. By picking a tree and not a mystical divine orb that stands outside of human jurisdiction, God places limits on human dominion. He has not given us a blank check. We must look to the creator for guidance in properly exercising dominion on his behalf.

Limits to Human Knowledge

Be that as it may, the Genesis author identifies this tree with knowledge of good and evil, and this, too, is intentional. Good and evil don't necessarily mean right and wrong. The phrase could be a merism—a pair of opposites on a particular continuum that are meant to represent the whole spectrum—in this case the whole range of human experience. In other words, humans have the ability to experience it all. But using such an ability is not always in our best interests.

It seems unlikely that God simply wanted humans to remain perpetually naïve and blind. But there are many ways of coming to know something. We can learn that something is bad for us by doing it and suffering the negative consequences. We can learn something by trusting the judgment of someone else who already knows. We can also learn by training our faculties to discern between good and evil (Heb 5:14). Like a good parent, the benevolent creator enlarges his creatures' capacity for knowledge when the time is right. Or, we can grow impatient and take the shortcut that this tree represents.

> **Urban Impatience**
>
> The last sentence in this section is poignant ... "Or, we can grow impatient and take the shortcut that this tree represents." While not addressing city building specifically there can be some direct applications as well as a multitude of examples where impatience has ruined many cities. We find this today in explosive suburbanization. While on one hand it created affordable housing for the middle class, now we're seeing more of the deleterious effects it has wrought on city dwellers. Most notably, an urban form that creates isolation, automobile dependency that hurts those financially vulnerable, and an uninspiring landscape. The most notable and beloved cities weren't rapidly put together in master-planned communities for maximum profit, but those that took a long time to develop.
>
> *Sean Benesh*

2:18-25 The Human Needs a Counterpart

A Strong Helper

The Genesis author has already established that the soil and the man need God and one another. But the man needs something more. It is not "good" for him to be alone. Apparently, God was not the ever-present garden companion that many people assume he once was. So the man needs a "helper as his partner." Chapter 1 presents creation's goodness every step of the way, ultimately culminating in the "very good" finished product. Chapter 2 slows down and emphasizes moments of deprivation that creation experienced along the way to its completion. At first there was no rain and no humans to tend to the soil. Now there are no animals and no fellow humans to accompany the man.

Scholars have convincingly demonstrated that the term "helper," in verse 18, does not imply subordination. God was not looking for an underling to serve the man, but a "strong helper" to be his counterpart.[33] "Strong helper" is a dynamic equivalent to the Hebrew word *ezer* in this verse. This term does not convey a sense of subordination, as the English term suggests. In fact, it is used quite frequently in verb and noun forms to refer to God in relationship to his people (Gen 2:49:25; Exod 18:4; Deut 33:7, 26, 29). He has the resources that humans lack, and he is uniquely positioned to help us out.

More specifically, the man needs a "helper *as his counterpart*." The Hebrew word for counterpart is *neged*, which means "opposite" or "corresponding part." This implies that man's helper is like him, but also different from him in a way that fits him—like adjacent pieces of a jigsaw puzzle. All the other animals have partners that are like them and ideally suit them. Male cats, dogs, and rabbits all have corresponding female cats, dogs, and rabbits without which they could not thrive as species.

This is not to say that each human is incomplete and requires an opposite gender soulmate to become whole. It is to say that a single human was not placed in charge of this world.[34] Rather, God gave dominion to a species that requires both genders to thrive and reproduce. Jesus certainly wasn't an incomplete human on account of having never married. Quite the opposite: in his singleness, he shows us what it means to be truly human. Yet Jesus was not a lonely or solitary man. Likeminded men and women were integral to his everyday life and ministry.

---

[33] For the term "strong helper," I am indebted to Nancy L. deClaissé-Walford, "Genesis 2: 'It is Not Good for the Human to Be Alone,'" *Review and Expositor* 103 (Spr 2006): 343-58.

[34] This could be a subtle critique of empire or kingship like the nations, perhaps anticipating the sons of God and Babel accounts (chs. 6 and 11, respectively).

Subordinate Animals

It is significant that before creating the woman, God created and paraded all the animals before the man. One might infer that this was intended to show that animals were inherently inferior to humans. It may, in fact, convey the opposite. In verse 7, God created the first human out of the ground to be a living being, a *nefesh*. Verse 19 says the same of animals. This should caution us against interpreting *nefesh* as "immortal soul" and reading a Greek body-soul dualism into the Genesis account.[35]

Nonetheless, the subordination of animals to humans is implied by this account. In the ancient world, naming someone was a way of exercising power over them. This passage depicts the man naming all the animals using the common Hebrew naming formula. This subordination of animals is important to chapter 3. It is worth noting that after the woman is created, the man does not name her using the same naming formula. He simply identifies her as also being what he is. He is an *ish* (a human) and she is an *isha* (a female human). This is one of the few places where parallel Hebrew terms translate nicely into English: man and woman. It is all the more significant, then, that the man uses the traditional naming formula to name the woman *after the Fall*—after God said that the man would rule over his woman (3:20). This is one of the strongest pieces of evidence that the man and woman functioned as equals before sin entered the world.

Sex and Marriage

Scholars have long speculated what it means that the woman was built out of the man's rib. The word for rib means "side." It is used multiple times in Exodus with reference to the side of the ark or tabernacle (*e.g.*, Exod 26:26). That the woman was taken from the man's side and

---

[35] See Lawson G. Stone, "The Soul: Possession, Part, or Person?" In *What About the Soul: Neuroscience* and *Christian Anthropology*, ed. Joel B. Green (Nashville: Abingdon, 2004), 47-61.

not his head or feet has long been interpreted as a statement of gender equality.[36] Ziony Zevit suggests that it refers to the man's baculum or penis bone (that which protrudes from his side). Many animals have such a bone, but not humans. He suggests that this story offers an etiology or origin account for why men lack such a bone and why they also have a distinct scar on the underside of their penis.[37] Since the text offers no additional clues, it is difficult to know exactly what the author had in mind.

The man is delighted with the woman that God built of and for him. He celebrates that what was once one flesh has become two. She is his genuine counterpart, the same flesh and bone. This sameness is celebrated in intercourse, when male and female become one flesh again. In Scripture, sex is *the* marital act. There is no such thing, biblically speaking, as pre- or extra-marital sex.[38] According to Jesus, sex is a real marital bond and it is a permanent one (Mark 10:2-12). It is little wonder that cultures which disconnect sex from marriage are deeply confused about sex. If churches today truly want to be a witness concerning marriage, they might begin by reconnecting sex and marriage and reclaiming the permanence of marriage in teaching and practice.

It is interesting to note, in verse 24, that in marriage it is the man who leaves his parents' household and cleaves to his wife. This is interesting because, in practice and throughout Genesis, women left their households and joined their husband's household (e.g., Rebekah, Rachel, and Leah).[39] It is tempting to think that this passage

---

[36] Nancy L. deClaissé-Walford, "Genesis 2," 343-58.

[37] Ziony Zevit, "Was Eve Made from Adam's Rib—or His Baculum," *Archaeology Review* 41, no. 5 (Sept/Oct 2015): 33-35; and *What Really Happened in the Garden of Eden* (New Haven, CT: Yale University Press, 2013), 140-50.

[38] Jacob learns this the hard way (Gen 29:21-27), as did certain Corinthians who solicited prostitutes (1 Cor 6:15-20).

advocates a matriarchal framework, but this is unlikely. There is little in later texts or Israelite practice to support this.

Perhaps this passage implies reciprocity. It goes without saying that women left their families behind, but men needed to be reminded to do the same and to build a genuinely new life together with their wives. They needed to be singled out because it would have been tempting for them to add their wives to their previous life as a sort of appendage. That temptation had to be resisted, especially in a world of polygamy. Such an interpretation makes sense in light of the unfolding narrative of Genesis. In chapter 3, husbands begin ruling over their wives; in chapter 4, Lamech appends two wives to himself; in chapter 6, the sons of God take wives as they see fit; and Abraham (ch. 20) and Isaac (ch. 26) both encounter kings that seek to enlarge their harems by taking wives from commoners.

Perhaps leaving parents is not about geography, but priority. The marital bond is supposed to be stronger than the blood bond with parents and siblings. In the West today, the challenge may be different. We are less tempted to prioritize our parents over our spouses and more tempted to prioritize our self, our friends, and our work.[40]

Or, perhaps, we are dealing with a translational error. Verse 24 may not be asking men to "leave" their parents at all. There is another Hebrew word with the same root letters that can mean restore, support, or strengthen (see Deut 22:4; Neh 3:8, 34). Were this the case, this passage would clarify that even though a man remains a support to

---

[39] Though Jacob spent quite a bit of time working for Rachel and Leah's father, the author narrates this as an undesirable situation that the overall plotline works to resolve.

[40] See Paul F. Scotchmer, "Lessons from Paradise on Work, Marriage, and Freedom: A Study of Genesis 2:4-3:24," *Evangelical Review of Theology* 28, 1 (Jan 2004): 80-85, esp. 82-83.

his parents, he clings to his wife in a unique and significant way.[41] Regardless of the precise meaning, Genesis 2 offers a strong statement about the nature and permanence of marriage that our world today desperately needs to see in practice.

---

[41] Zevit, "What Really Happened," 153-57.

FALL AND AFTERMATH 3:1—6:4

Fall: 3:1-24

Genesis 3, traditionally referred to as the Fall account, provides important background information for our understanding of what God is doing in world history. It famously recounts what is wrong with this world and how it got this way. Had the Fall not happened, it is not clear God would have ever needed to form a set apart people and send them into the world in mission.

Like the first two chapters, this one is riddled with questions and controversies. I will focus on three of them. Who was the serpent and what were his motives for instigating the Fall? Did God really walk and talk with humans in the garden? What were the consequences of sin and how much should we allow them to define reality for us?

3:1-7 Creatures Conspire against God

The Serpent's Identity

In recent years, the gap between the consensus of scholars and the beliefs of the average Christian has been shrinking. This is, in part, due to the average person's instant access to scholarly opinions and arguments by way of the internet. Yet when it comes to the identity of the serpent, a large gap still remains. Many Bible scholars have been working with the notion that the serpent is what the text says he is: the shrewdest of the animals God created. Still, for most Christians and a good number of theologians, the serpent is the Devil.

It is worth briefly considering the contours of this debate since the outcome often colors one's perception of sin and God's efforts in dealing with it. We should acknowledge from the outset that nothing in Genesis 3 associates the Devil with the serpent. The word "Devil" or "Satan" is not used. Verse 1 identifies the serpent in connection with the animals. And God does not engage the serpent as if he were the Devil but curses him using language that continues to associate him with the animals: "cursed are you among all animals and among all wild creatures" (v. 14). What is more, the Devil is strikingly absent from the rest of Genesis and indeed the overwhelming majority of the Old Testament.[42]

Why then do many people identify the serpent as the Devil? Perhaps because the New Testament seems to do so. He is called the "father of lies" in John 8:44, God crushes him under believers' feet in Romans 6:20, and he is equated with an "ancient serpent" in Revelation 12:9-15 and 20:2. Though the passages in John and Romans would serve as helpful corroborative evidence, they are not overt enough to establish a sure connection. Some of the language in these passages could refer to Genesis 3:3, but that is far from certain.

The Revelation passages seem to be a slam dunk. The Devil and Satan are identified as "that ancient serpent" and, as the story of Revelation begins to wrap up in chapter 22, humans regain access to the tree of life (vv. 2, 14, 19), which they previously lost because they listened to the serpent in Genesis 3. What could be more clear? Yet this evidence is deceiving. Before we link two characters in any story we must consider the similarities between them, the dissimilarities, and the possibility that some other character may fit the description better.

The dissimilarities are noteworthy. The beast in Revelation is a flying dragon with seven heads. It is associated with water and flood, and it battles against angels and humans. By way of contrast, the Genesis serpent has one head (Gen 3:15), is forced to crawl on the ground, is associated with dust, and is the lowest of animals.[43] Those wishing to link

---

[42] Notable exceptions include 1 Chronicles 21:1; Job 1 & 2; and Zechariah 3. Some thinkers also identify Satan with the "day star" of Isaiah 14:12 and the king of Tyre in Ezekiel 28.

[43] It is also noteworthy that the serpent is said to have offspring

the serpent with the dragon must give an account for how the serpent overcame divine subjugation to become a glorious beast with tremendous power. The Bible offers no such account. This should be enough to raise doubts.

Equally important, another candidate better fits the description of the beast in Revelation. Several Old Testament books refer to a mythological creature called Leviathan (Job 3:8; 41:1; Ps 74:12-17; 104:26; Isa 27:1) and sometimes Rahab (Job 26:12; Ps 89:10; Isa 51:9). Leviathan is a primordial creature symbolizing the chaos that God defeated while bringing order to this world at the time of creation. This is, of course, not how Genesis depicts creation. Rather Job, Psalms, and Isaiah draw upon Ugaritic mythology where such is the case. Their point is not to endorse the truthfulness of these ancient myths, but to show the superiority of Israel's God over the gods of Canaanite mythology.

Isaiah 27 pertains to Revelation for multiple reasons. First, Isaiah is one of the books that Revelation draws from most heavily. Just like it borrows "tree of life" imagery from Genesis 2-3, so it borrows "new heavens and earth" imagery from Isaiah 65.[44] Second, Isaiah 24-27 is often called the "apocalypse of Isaiah." Like Revelation, it is apocalyptic in nature. This is important because one of the characteristics of apocalypses is that they borrow and recycle imagery from earlier apocalypses.

Most important, Revelation 12 closely parallels Isaiah 27:1, which reads, "On that day the LORD with his cruel and great and strong sword will punish Leviathan the fleeing serpent, Leviathan the twisting serpent, and he will kill the dragon that is in the sea." The language "on that day" is

---

(Gen 3:15), but the Devil is never said to have offspring.

[44] Revelation borrows heavily from Isaiah in numerous other places. See Jan Fekkes, *Isaiah and Prophetic Traditions in the Book of Revelation: Visionary Antecedents and their Development*, Journal for the study of the New Testament Supplement series 93 (Sheffield, England: JSOT Press, 1994).

eschatological. It points to what the seer anticipates happening in the future when God intervenes in world history to set things straight. Revelation envisions this same day. The Leviathan of Isaiah is also described, like the beast in Revelation, as a serpent *and* a dragon. Isaiah 27 is not describing two different beasts: one that is a serpent and another that is a dragon. Rather, using synonymous parallelism—the defining feature of Hebrew poetry—the author employs two terms to describe the same creature.

Most noteworthy, this passage refers to Leviathan as a "fleeing serpent" and a "twisting serpent." This makes unambiguously clear that the author is borrowing imagery from the Baal cycles of Canaanite mythology. These myths, which predate the book of Isaiah and are native to Palestine, describe Baal's victory over a primordial beast called Lotan using identical language: "When you smite *Lotan* the *fleeing serpent*, finish off the *twisting serpent*, the close-coiling one with seven heads."[45]

Lotan is Ugaritic for *Leviathan*. Ugaritic and Hebrew are sister languages, and in those languages these names share the same consonants. That Isaiah uses this name and describes his beast as a "fleeing" and "twisting" "serpent" leaves no doubt that they refer to the same creature. It is all the more significant, then, that this creature has seven heads, just like the beast in Revelation.

Which text better parallels Revelation's depiction of a beast? Genesis, which has an ancient serpent who is associated with mischief—or Isaiah, which has an ancient dragon serpent with seven heads that is associated with mischief that God is expected to overcome at the end of time? The answer is clearly Isaiah. This severely weakens the New Testament basis for identifying the garden serpent with the Devil.

---

[45] Eds. William W. Hallow and K. Lawson Younger, *The Context of Scripture*, vol. 1 (Leiden: Brill, 2002), 265.

The Serpent's Motive

One strength of the Devil theory is that it provides ready answers to intriguing questions. How could the serpent talk? How did the serpent know that the humans would not die immediately after eating the fruit? How did it know they would become like God? Why would it even want to tempt the humans? If we assume the Devil did it, we can see throughout the rest of the Bible that the Devil appears to have superhuman knowledge and ability, and he delights in leading humans astray. Yet Genesis does not supply the serpent's motive.

The first book on record that links the Genesis serpent to the Devil and attributes a specific motive to him is the pseudepigraphal book, *The Life of Adam and Eve*. We cannot date this work with precision, but it may have been written as early as the first century CE. It appears to be a Jewish work rather than Christian, since it associates the resurrection of the dead with the seventh day and not the first (51:23). It also espouses Greek mythological views such as the cleansing of the soul in Lake Archeron and the migration of souls to heaven. It should not be counted among more mainstream apocryphal and pseudepigraphal works (like Sirach and 1 Enoch), which were deemed by some to be canonical. Still, it appears to have had a profound impact on the interpretation of the Fall account.

In *The Life of Adam and Eve*, the serpent was a fallen angel who tempted Eve out of a desire for revenge (11:2—16:3). As the story goes, when God created Adam he commanded the angels in heaven to bow before Adam since he was made in God's image. One of the angels, Satan, would not humble himself in this way. He refused to bow and he threatened to raise his own throne above God. So God cast him out of heaven, along with his rebellious companions. Having lost everything, the Devil sought to avenge himself by instigating a breach between humans and God. He then convinced a serpent to allow him to possess his body. The rest is history.

As indicated earlier, many scholars reject this interpretation. They posit a variety of theories that begin with the belief that the serpent was simply an animal:

1. The jealous serpent theory takes as its point of departure the idea that the serpent was the wisest creature. That being the case, it would have been "runner up" to the woman as the first man's ideal companion. Out of jealousy or perhaps the bitterness of being rejected, the serpent sought to disrupt the happy harmony that humans were enjoying.[46]

2. The *fearful serpent theory* also begins by assuming that the serpent had a closer relationship with Adam than all the other animals. Upon discovering that the woman was chosen as the man's ideal counterpart, the serpent feared that its relationship with the man would never be the same. The woman would monopolize Adam's affections and literally leave the serpent in the dust. So it intentionally compromised their superior bond by instigating the Fall.[47]

3. The *obedient serpent theory* holds that God willed for humans to gain knowledge of good and evil. He wanted them to eat from the tree eventually. The serpent simply carried out God's wishes and should not be deemed an agent with malicious intent.[48]

4. The *eco-friendly serpent theory* also affirms that God wanted humans to eat from the tree and eventually leave the garden. It focuses on why humans must leave the garden. Since God intended humans to serve the

---

[46] Lawson G. Stone, "The Soul: Possession, Part, or Person?" In *What About the Soul: Neuroscience and Christian Anthropology*, ed. Joel B. Green (Nashville: Abingdon, 2004), 47-61.

[47] Zevit, *What Really Happened*, 165-66. This book is one of the most interesting and provocative recent treatments of the Eden story.

[48] Judith E. McKinlay, "Bothering to Enter the Garden of Eden Once Again," *Feminist Theology* 19, no. 2 (Dec 2010): 143-153.

soil and not themselves, they needed to move beyond Eden to serve all soil throughout the whole earth. The serpent was simply God's instrument for triggering their worldwide creation-serving mandate.[49]

All of these approaches have merit, though some do not take seriously enough the punishment that God metes out to the serpent. The consequences it must face imply strongly that the serpent was at least partly wrong.[50]

I am not sure I have *the* answer, but I would like to suggest a speculative scenario that also takes as its point of departure that the serpent was an animal: the *curious calculating serpent theory*. To begin with, we must reckon with the serpent's advanced knowledge. It is not only wiser than all other animals, but it appears to be wiser than the humans. It imparts truth when it says that humans will not die upon eating the fruit, but will become like God. They did not die on the day they ate, and God confirms that eating the fruit has made them like him (3:22).

The intriguing part is how the serpent came to know these things. One seldom-explored possibility is that it had already eaten the fruit.[51] Having done so, it knew firsthand that death does not immediately follow. Furthermore, it may have personally experienced an increase of God-like knowledge. Were this the case, the serpent could have been genuinely inquisitive as he approached the woman. Would she really die? Why would God not want her to eat of it?

---

[49] Arthur Walker-Jones, "Eden for Cyborgs: Ecocriticism and Genesis 2-3," *Biblical Interpretation* 16 (2008): 263-293.

[50] Zevit is more consistent in that he interprets none of the consequence of the Fall as punitive (chs. 19-21). Though I don't find this convincing, it is internally coherent.

[51] I owe this insight to Deborah Delcamp a fellow church member who raised this possibility during a Bible study, as well as Heather Bunce, another member of Delta Community Christian Church, who tested this possibility in a seminary research paper.

This, of course, was a dangerous risk. The serpent may have continued to live after partaking because God never forbade the serpent from partaking. As an animal, it was not created in God's image and did not receive dominion over the earth. It was morally unaccountable. If the prohibition against eating from the tree represented a limitation that God placed on human dominion, then that limitation need not apply to other creatures. Moral accountability comes only with responsibility.

It is an interesting feature of creaturely existence that animals are not morally accountable. They routinely steal what others worked for, and they enjoy intercourse with a wide variety of partners. That is the ordinary state of most species. Of course, humans try to domesticate many animals, which opens up the possibility that they transgress their trainers' will. But in God's sight—as far as we can tell—animals are morally free. A possible exception to this is that God later holds animals accountable for bloodshed (Gen 9:5). Still, that may be more about upholding the sanctity of human life than establishing the reality of animal morality.

We cannot be sure that the serpent knew about the moral distinction between humans and animals. If it did know—whether from eating or from conversations with the humans—then perhaps its motive was a matter of "status envy" before God. As the wisest subhuman, it was second only to humans. Since there was no way to manipulate a promotion out of God, it may have sought to engineer the demotion of humans. It invites humans to act as if they, too, were morally unaccountable. For them to do so might bring them down to the serpent's level, which is the best it could do to elevate its status.

Careful analysis of 4:13-19 suggests that each consequence of sin in some way counteracts a specific motivation or circumstance behind the sin. If I am right about this, the fact that God makes the serpent the lowest animal may suggest that its motivation was to become the highest—even above humans. Before considering these verses in detail, we return one last time to the theme of God's presence in the garden.

3:8-24 Consequences for Disobedience

> **Root Causes of Brokenness**
>
> If there ever was a root of the ailments that every city faces it is found here in Genesis 3:8-24. While sociologists, economists, politicians, urban planners, and the like point out and note what is wrong or broken about their cities, the root causes bring us back to this account in Genesis. This is key as it gives us perspective when it comes to our involvement in the city. The root causes of brokenness in our cities are not faltering economies, oppressive governments, soul-sucking urban form, racial tension and the like ... it is sin. This list then simply represents the symptoms of this deeper issue. That means our work in the city is both spiritual and physical. At the same time, we seek to fight racism or economic exclusion we have before us the privilege of introducing people to the life-giving Savior and life in his kingdom.
>
> Sean Benesh

The Divine Walk

In contrast to chapter 1, where God simply speaks forth and creation unfolds, Genesis 2-3 stands out in how the creator draws near to his creation. He is called by the more intimate name "Yahweh God." He molds the first human from clay. He teaches them what to do and not to do in the garden. And, perhaps most famously, he walks in the garden before confronting human disobedience. There is no denying that the transcendent God of chapter 1 has drawn near to his creatures in chapters 2-3. But is there truly enough evidence to suggest that humans and God enjoyed one another's company in a casual or recreational sense?

God's walk in the garden is often presented as the strongest evidence that Eden was a place of regular divine-human interaction. As one author puts it, "God casually strolls, enjoying the company of the garden's denizens."[52] Others speak of this passage as evidence that God "communed with them"[53] or regularly spent the cool of the day "just strolling with Adam and Eve."[54] From the fact that God asks where Adam is, another author infers that God regularly met with the gardener and his helpmeet in that particular place, "perhaps to talk over what had to be done on the morrow."[55]

Yet all of that is inference. Quite literally, all that Genesis 3:8 says is that "they heard the sound of the LORD God walking [back and forth] in the wind of the day and then they hid." God is the only one walking, and there is no hint of casual fellowship. All we know is that, on this particular day, the humans heard a sound that they were able to identify as God, and that caused them to hide. When God finds them, he interrogates them, states the consequences of their misdeeds, and expels them.

This verse is so cryptic that Jeffrey Niehaus suggests that it depicts a divine judgment scene. He interprets the "wind" as a storm, the "sound" as God's thundering presence, and the "walking to and fro" as God's furious pacing.[56]

---

[52] William P. Brown, "Manifest Diversity: The Presence of God in Genesis," in *Genesis and Christian Theology*, 3-25, eds. Nathan MacDonald, Mark W. Elliott, and Grant Macaskill (Grand Rapids: Eerdmans, 2012), 2.

[53] Craig G. Bartholomew and Michael W. Goheen, *The Drama of Scripture: Finding Our Place in the Biblical Story* (Grand Rapids: Bakers, 2004), 42.

[54] Wright, *The Mission of God*, 334.

[55] Zevit, *What Really Happened*, 177.

[56] Jeffrey Niehaus, "In the Wind of the Storm," *Vetus Testamentum* 46 (1994): 263-267.

The Hebrew term for "walk" in verse 8 is in the reflexive form, which means something like "walking back and forth." When this form applies to an event that spans a long period of time, it suggests that the action happened on a regular basis. In this sense, God "walked among" his people in the tabernacle over many years (Lev 26:12). He was not always present, but he came and went periodically. That is why many scholars infer from this word that God regularly walked in the garden.

Genesis 3:8 does not describe God's practice over a long period of time. It describes the sound that the guilt-ridden humans heard at a particular time and place. In such a limited context, the reflexive form indicates something that repeatedly moves back and forth. We don't have to look far to see a perfect example of this. After God expels humans from the garden, he places a flaming sword "flashing back and forth" (NIV) to keep people out of the garden (3:24). The term for "flashing back and forth" is a single word in Hebrew that occurs in the reflexive form. When not in the reflexive form, it simply means "to turn."

With this in mind, we should translate the term for "walk" in 3:8 as "walking back and forth." The wind was blowing, God was walking back and forth, the humans heard it, and they hid. It may be that the language of this verse is not strong enough to convey a full-blown storm theophany,[57] but even less does it convey intimate communion with God. We cannot assume that because humans recognize the sound as God that he must have visited with them on a regular basis. Perhaps Adam remembered the sound from when God told him to name the animals. Or perhaps it was so extraordinary and powerful that they assumed it was God, especially because they expected to hear from him concerning their act of disobedience.

---

[57] Christopher L. K. Grundke argues against Niehaus's thesis in "A Tempest in a Teapot? Genesis III 8 Again," *Vetus Testamentum* 51, no. 4 (2001): 548-551. Grundke does not deal with the fact that Genesis 3 never associates garden expulsion with separation from God's presence.

The bottom line is that the garden scene does not furnish an adequate basis for asserting that God and humans once enjoyed intimate life together in Eden. To be sure, God occasionally approached and spoke with them, but God does this sort of thing uninterrupted all throughout Genesis. He speaks with Cain and gives him a mark (ch. 4). He speaks with Noah, instructs him to build the ark, and afterward gives him regulations for human thriving (chs. 6-9). He speaks with Abraham multiple times and even shares a meal with him (ch. 18). He engages Jacob in a prolonged wrestling match (ch. 22). When it comes to immediate physical interactions between humans and God, the Fall account doesn't appear to be a game changer. This is not to say that God's relationship with humans hasn't changed—only that divine presence isn't the issue.

Consequences of Irresponsibility

If intimate fellowship with God were a staple of garden existence, then separation from God's presence would certainly be named among the devastating consequences of sin and banishment from the garden. It is therefore quite telling that it is not. Instead, the author focuses entirely on the new status of his creatures, how they relate to one another, and their separation from the tree of life.[58]

The consequences of human irresponsibility were disastrous for the entire created order. God's approach to their disobedience is noteworthy. He confronts Adam first, which may indicate that Adam is most responsible for this offense. We are not told that this has anything to do with his maleness. We are only told that God delivered the prohibition against eating from the tree of knowledge directly to him (2:17). God also holds the woman responsible. After Adam passes the buck her way, God questions her as to what happened. She, in turn, blames

---

[58] Most of what follows in my commentary on vv. 8-24 is taken, nearly verbatim, from my book *Endangered Gospel: How Fixing the World is Killing the Church* (Eugene, OR: Cascade Books, 2016), 34-37.

the serpent. Interestingly, God does not engage the serpent in conversation. This must have been a terrible blow to its ego. The serpent failed to achieve human-level status after all. God refused to dignify its manipulative attempt at self-promotion by addressing it in a humanlike way.

Nonetheless, all parties suffer the consequences: the responsible humans, the non-responsible accomplice, and the inanimate accessory. The consequences are of two sorts. One is a natural outcome of the choice to sin. It is not something that God initiates. Rather, humans trigger it by choosing sin. The other is a divine action that brings about a specific change in creaturely existence. This action is often as much gracious initiative as it is punishment.

It is helpful to distinguish between the natural outcomes and gracious initiatives. God's pronouncement in Genesis 3 is not the beginning of a string of wrath-filled actions that an angry God unleashes upon his wayward creatures. It is not as if God first curses the original sinners, next floods the earth, then annihilates the Canaanites, and eventually everyone else who rubs him the wrong way. One does not have to be a Jew or a Christian to see that this sort of interpretation gets the story all wrong.

Notice that after God expels Adam and Eve from the garden, he sews clothing for them and helps Eve bear their first child (4:1). Notice that after Cain kills his brother Abel, God protects Cain from those who would kill him in an effort to make the world a safer place (4:15). Notice that God was grieved by the sin that required him to flood the earth—not infuriated by humans and ready to unleash his pent-up fury (6:6).

God's poetic declaration in Genesis 3 contains both a description of the mess humans made of God's world *and* a description of how God begins to clean up that mess through strategic countermoves that preserve his original purposes for creation. The contributions humans make are stated as matters of fact. God's countermoves are sometimes, but not always stated in the language of curses.

The Serpent

God's first countermove is to curse the serpent by demoting it to its belly (v. 14). It is now the lowest of all creatures. This demotion in status may indicate that God perceived the serpent's motive to be an elevation in status. This is bad for the serpent's agenda, but good for humans. An enlarged gap between humans and animals ensures that these two parties will no longer conspire together against God's authority. Should humans sin again, it won't be because the serpent made them do it.

The relational proximity that allowed an animal to lead humans astray is replaced with enmity. Animals—especially snakes—will strike at human heels and inflict injury, and humans will ultimately triumph over them (v. 15). It's not as if God instigates every skirmish between humans and animals. God does not throw humans and creatures in a cage together, sound a bell, and then watch them tear each other apart. Rather, because of sin, the harmony that once existed between all creatures was seriously disrupted, and it has been this way ever since. God enlarged the gap between humans and animals for our own good, and we lash out against one another without divine provocation.

The Woman

God then acts by increasing the pain women experience in childbirth (v. 16). Curse language is not used here as with the serpent. God had something else in mind. The dispute that led to human independence from God had to do with life and death. God warned that eating from the forbidden tree would lead to death. By placing the tree of life in the garden, God gave humans and perhaps other creatures the opportunity to enjoy life without end. Eve weighed the benefits of eating the forbidden fruit against the risk. She then chose knowledge and the possibility of death.

Like the serpent's status violation, this choice required a divine corrective. God institutes a painful gestation period for humans, followed by high risk labor and delivery.

Though this could be interpreted as mere punishment, it also instilled in humans a deeper appreciation for the gift of life. Human existence is not like an annual cycle of crops that may be reaped in large quantities on a cyclical basis. Life is precious and fragile, not to be taken for granted. It is worth the cost of respecting the limits that God places on our dominion. Morning sickness, miscarriages, dying mothers, and various forms of infant mortality have been with us ever since.

The next consequence of sin is not presented as a divine initiative. God tells Eve that her *desire* will be for her husband and that he will *rule over* her (v. 16). God does not say, "I will make you desire your husband and command him to rule over you." The sentence is not constructed that way in the original language. Importantly, the words for "desire" and "rule" have many connotations, some positive, some negative. Significantly, these same words are used in the very next chapter (Gen 4). There they describe sin's *desire* to overtake Cain and Cain's need to *rule over* it (v. 7). It is most likely, then, that God is warning Eve that her choice to sin has created a world of conflict between men and women. Unfortunately for her gender, men will typically dominate that relationship. Most women can only long for that sort of power. Eve inadvertently traded the equal dominion of Genesis 1-2 for a battle of the sexes that women often lose.

God did not instigate this. Rather, sin created a world in which shared leadership is rare and those with more power rule over those with less. This means not only the fall of women from power, but the fall of power into domination.[59] The rich will dominate the poor, the strong will dominate

---

[59] For this insight, I am indebted to John Howard Yoder, "Feminist Theology Miscellany #1: Salvation Through Mothering?" (April 1988), available in the John Howard Yoder Digital Library at http://palni.contentdm.oclc.org/cdm/landingpage/collection/p15705co ll18 See also, Yoder, *The End of Sacrifice: The Capital Punishment Writings of John Howard Yoder*, ed. John C. Nugent (Harrisonburg, VA: Herald Press, 2011), ch. 5, pt. 6.

the weak, and humans will dominate animals and exploit creation. In most cases, the weaker party longs for the power of the stronger. God does not sanction this state of affairs; he simply warns that it is the new terrain that all creatures must now navigate.

The Man

When God addresses Adam, he refrains from cursing him directly. Instead, he curses the ground. The decision to eat the forbidden fruit transgressed the limits of human dominion and depreciated the value of human life. It also disdained the abundant provisions that God supplied for humans. Adam and Eve lacked nothing in Eden. Though they had endless rations, they did not consider them enough. They wanted it all. They spurned the gift of food, just like the gift of life.

So God initiates another corrective: he curses the soil that sustained the tree that produced the fruit that served as an accessory to sin. It no longer yields fruit in abundance. Humans must toil arduously to harvest a decent crop. The superior strength that gives men an upper hand in power struggles with women also equips them best to break through the newly hardened soil. Of course, women and animals bear this burden as well. No aspect of creation is immune from the mess that sin has made of this world.

The ultimate consequence of sin is death. The dust out of which God created Adam becomes the tomb of human death and decay. God banishes humans from the garden, which was their only access to the tree of life. Death is now an ongoing reality. This, too, was a divine initiative, and so a measure of grace. To live forever in a state of sin could itself be a form of torture. Eternal enmity with the animal kingdom, eternal scratching at hardened soil, eternal domination of the strong over the weak—none of this is what God had in mind for this world. By ending life in a sin-spoiled world, God creates the necessity and therefore the possibility of a new beginning. The conditions for God's mission in this world were beginning to take shape.

Aftermath of the Fall: Genesis 4:1—6:4

Overly simplistic tellings of the Bible story often begin with Genesis 1-3 and emphasize how sin caused the fall of God's good creation. It is then common for people to skip to the New Testament to highlight how Jesus conquered sin and began to reverse the negative consequences of sin. Genesis 4 thus serves as the beginning point of the all too frequent eclipse of the Old Testament. Much is lost from this sort of approach, since chapters 4-11 are crucial for putting flesh on God's skeletal summary of sin's negative consequences in chapter 3. These eight chapters illustrate for us what it means for men to struggle with cursed soil, women to struggle with male dominance, animals to suffer from human violence, and all of creation to grapple with the reality of death.

4:1-8 Brother Murders Brother

Eve's Predominance

The first consequence of sin we encounter in chapter 4 is painful childbirth.[60] In verse 1, we are told that Adam "knew" or had intercourse with Eve who conceives and bears a son. Adam then recedes deeply into the background. All he does from this point forward is beget Seth and die at a ripe old age (4:25; 5:3-5). Eve, on the other hand, gives birth to Cain, credits God—not Adam—for helping her, takes the lead in naming Cain, gives birth to two more sons, and personally names Seth (4:25).

What should we make of Eve's relative prominence over Adam in this account? Is it incidental, or was it meant to reflect the power struggle that God previously claimed would beset spousal relations? Consider the evidence. In 4:25, we are told unambiguously that Eve names Seth. It is the same naming formula that describes Adam's naming of

---

[60] We are not told specifically that Eve suffered much while giving birth, but she goes out of her way in v. 1 to acknowledge God's help.

Eve in 3:20. In that context, as previously noted, the man appears to be asserting his newly discovered rule over his wife. So, in naming her son, is Eve asserting her own rule over a man? Is this an expression of her "desire" (3:16) for her man's power, which she asserts as soon as she has the opportunity?

Interestingly, Eve declares in 4:1 that she has produced a "man" with the help of God.[61] She does not say she gave birth to a human (*adam*, cf. 5:2), offspring (*zerah*, cf. 4:25), children (*banin*, cf. 3:16), or even a son (*ben*, cf. 4:17)—but to a man (*ish*, cf. 2:23-24). Such language is unexpected and is not used elsewhere in quite the same way. In Genesis 3-4, this word for man is most often used to distinguish between male and female spouses. In 3:16, it identifies the male spouse who will rule over his wife as a consequence of sin.

It is thus significant that Eve claims to have produced a "man" and then proceeds to name him. The Hebrew word translated "produce" in 4:1 (NRSV) is a deliberate play on the word "Cain." Such puns are standard practice in naming formulas. In the previous chapter, Adam names his wife "Eve," which sounds like the world for "life," because she is the mother of "all living" (3:20). Since Eve is the one doing the producing with the help of God—and not Adam—it makes the most sense that Eve did the naming, as she later does with Seth (4:25). Such man naming appears to be a deliberate effort to assert her leadership as a woman, perhaps to offset her husband's increasing power over her.

This interpretation is reinforced by the fact that, whereas the narrator informs us that Adam is the father of Cain and Seth, in both instances Eve emphasizes her connection and

---

[61] The Apostle Paul appears to agree that women bringing forth male children neutralizes the power imbalance that some people in Corinth appear to have rooted in the fact that men were created first (1 Cor 11:8-12). This may explain why, in 1 Timothy, Paul encourages women to bear children after noting the power imbalance generated by creation order (2:13-15).

dependence upon *God* for her sons (4:1; 5:25). Adam doesn't seem to be involved with his sons; Eve and God do all the naming and advising.

This interpretation may go a long way to clarifying a particularly confusing New Testament passage. In her role as mother and in the act of naming a man, Eve regained some of the status and power that she lost when her sin helped create a world in which men dominate over women. This rebalancing of power through childbearing may be what Paul was referring to when he told certain women that they will be "saved [restored] through childbearing" (1 Tim 2:15) and not by lording over men at church.[62] Salvation here is not about establishing a right relationship with God. No human work can accomplish this, except for the work of Christ. Salvation for women, in this passage, is likely about them experiencing in tangible ways their newfound equality in Christ (2 Cor 5:16-17; Gal 3:28). Usurping power from men, as some were attempting to do (1 Tim 2:12), was not the answer. Striving for more power is what led Eve to sin in the first place (Gen 3:4-6). Rather, drawing upon the serving, protecting, nurturing leadership of childrearing paves a better way forward and prepares women for the kind of leadership that Jesus taught and that the church really needs.[63]

---

[62] I am indebted to John Howard Yoder for this insight. For further details, see Nugent, *The Politics of Yahweh: John Howard Yoder, the Old Testament, and the People of God* (Eugene, OR: Cascade Books, 2011), 26-28; Yoder, *The End of Sacrifice*, 192-195.

[63] This places in clearer perspective Paul's appeal to Eve in 1 Tim 2:14. Paul advocated a strong connection between church leadership and household management (1 Tim 3:5 and 3:12). So, if these women want to grow into influential church leaders, they should begin by becoming exemplary leaders in the household context, which many troublemaking women were clearly not doing (4:11-14). Elsewhere, moreover, Paul forthrightly states that women bringing forth male children neutralizes the power imbalance that some people rooted in the fact that men were created first (1 Cor 11:8-12). This helps explain why, in 1 Timothy 2, he encourages women to bear children immediately after noting the power imbalance generated by creation order (vv. 13-15). Read in this light,

Cain's Insecurity

After Eve names Cain, we are told that she births a second son named Abel (4:2). We are not told that she names Abel. It may be that Abel receives the name we know him by only later. His name literally means vapor, mist, or breath. It is the same word that the teacher uses in Ecclesiastes when he says "meaningless, meaningless, everything is meaningless" (1:2). It is meaningless because, like vapor or mist, one cannot get a solid grip on life. As soon as people think they do, it slips right through their fingers. How fitting that short-lived Abel would be remembered by a name that refers to that which does not last.

We hear nothing of Cain and Abel's childhood play. The account turns directly to their respective occupations. Abel keeps sheep, and Cain works the soil. At some point, both sons offer God a portion of their life's work. God appreciates Abel's offering, but not that of Cain. Cain is discouraged by this, so God encourages him to find acceptance by doing well (v. 7). He also warns that, if Cain does not do well, sin is poised to overcome him. Interestingly, the same language is used of sin's relationship with Cain and the woman's newly compromised relationship with her husband: "its *desire* is for you, but you must *master* it" (4:7; cf. 3:16). This means, at the very least, that gender tension is not a desirable state of affairs. Like sin, it is a destructive force at work in this world. Of course, Cain did not heed God's warning. He gave sin a foothold, allowed jealousy to consume him, and led his brother out to the field to kill him (v. 8).

Paul was not telling women simply to raise kids and let men do all the leading. Rather, he was encouraging women who wanted to lead, but weren't ready to lead and were going about it in all the wrong ways, that they have to start in the same place as male leaders, which is to be exemplary leaders at home. He wasn't permanently barring women from church leadership but training them for church leadership in a way that was appropriate to his first century context.

Scholars have long debated why God looked upon Abel's offering with favor and not that of Cain. The simplest explanation is that Abel gave the "firstlings" and "fat portions" of his flock (v. 4), whereas Cain simply gave a portion of his crops (v. 3). Abel gave his best, whereas Cain gave the bare minimum. We learn in Torah that God requires the Israelites to give only their best.[64] Though simplicity is preferable in many cases, this explanation appears notably disconnected from the rest of the immediate narrative.

It is worth considering additional factors. One is the specific occupations of the brothers. As a farmer, Cain was required to work the soil that God had cursed in the previous chapter. His occupation would therefore be a continual reminder of sin's painful consequences. He had to dig, scrape, and scratch the earth to wrest from it the basic sustenance by which humans live. As a shepherd, Abel's relationship to the soil and flock was quite different. Shepherds give relatively free reign to their flocks and allow them to move about in search of vegetation that is growing of its own accord. Cain's occupation was conflictual; Abel's was cooperative. Cain worked against the curse; Abel worked around it.[65]

This is not a moral judgment. It is a statement of reality. In a fallen world, both occupations were valuable and necessary for human survival. Still, one was more at peace with God's creation and thus the recipient of divine favor and blessing.[66] It could be that God blessed Abel with

---

[64] Exod 34:26; Lev 3:3; Num 18:29-32; Deut 12:5-6.

[65] Joel Litke goes further to say that shepherding fosters habits of caring for the flock and spending time with God, whereas farming fosters pride in self-accomplishment to the extent that farmers must master and manipulate the soil to yield what they will. See Litke, "The Message of Chapter 4 of Genesis," *Jewish Biblical Quarterly* 31, no. 3 (July-Sept 2003): 197-200.

[66] See John Howard Yoder, "On Generating Alternative

abundant flocks all throughout the year in a way that he did not bless Cain and his crops. Perhaps this is what it means for God to have "regard for Abel and his offering" (v. 4). Were this the case, Cain was bitter that he had so little to show for all his hard work—and it wasn't even his fault![67] As firstborn son, he inherited the occupation of his father.[68] Abel, on the other hand, simply took up the work that his older brother left undone. This may anticipate God's tendency later in Genesis to overlook firstborn sons, as we see with Abraham and his near descendants.

Whatever this passage means, it must make sense in light of God's statement that if Cain "does well" he will be accepted and, if not, sin will overtake him (v. 7). It seems unlikely that doing well means becoming a shepherd like his brother. It could mean offering his best crops, but it could also mean remaining faithful in his farming and not holding it against his brother that God blesses him in a unique way. This is a lesson that Esau will later have to learn.[69]

Coveting God's favor is no less a problem for God's people today, whether we covet the abilities of fellow believers, the influence of Christian leaders, or the success of other ministries. If we continue to do well with what God has given us, where he has planted us, he will indeed accept us. Nothing else matters. Anything more can be deadly.

Paradigms," in *Human Values and the Environment: Conference Proceedings* 140 (Madison, WI: Wisconsin Academy of Science, Arts, and Letters, 1992), 57-59.

[67] Gunther Wittenberg, "Alienation and 'Emancipation' from the Earth: The Earth Story in Genesis 4," in *The Earth Story in Genesis*, eds. Norman C. Habel and Shirley Wurst (Sheffield: Sheffield Academic Press, 2000), 107.

[68] Wittenberg, "Alienation and Emancipation," 107.

[69] When Esau leaves Jacob (the favored one) alone, rather than kill him as he intended, God prospers Esau with a large family and army (Gen 32-33). Still, Jacob is blessed in a way that Esau will never be.

4:9-16 Consequences for Murder

> **Murder, Exile, and Protection**
>
> This account sets up the backstory of what happens next: the founding of the first recorded city in Scripture. Before we jump to the next section, it is paramount to note what happens here after Cain murders Abel. In the midst of Abel's murder and Cain's resultant exile, God still extends grace to Cain. For the modern reader, this may seem like a lack of justice. The thought of Cain's punishment as simply geographic exile along with a severed relationship with God seems underwhelming. However, God is both just and gracious. In the midst of murder and exile there is grace and even protection extended.
>
> This represents a healthy pattern for cities. Offenses should be dealt with appropriately and accordingly. At the same time there should be grace and hope for offenders. Life is valuable. This creates much tension. How much is too much punishment? At the same time how much is too much grace? Cities need a balance of both justice and grace to dwell in the middle of this tension and to ensure health and wellness for their citizens.
>
> *Sean Benesh*

Readers often overestimate the extent to which banishment from Eden meant separation from God's presence. We already noted how God helped Eve give birth to a son. And now, just like he did in the garden, God approaches a wayward human about his death-dealing sin. Only, this time, instead of asking the man, "Where are you?" he asks, "Where is your brother Abel?"

Cain responds quite differently. Whereas Adam quickly spills his beans (3:10), Cain lies to God and claims that he doesn't know Abel's whereabouts. He then asks the rather snarky question, "Am I my brother's keeper?" (4:9). This is a clever play on words. Abel was introduced as a "keeper" of sheep (v. 2). In essence, Cain retorts, "Does the shepherd need a shepherd?"

Like with Adam, God follows up with another question, which is probably more of an exclamation: "What have you done?!" Instead of waiting for an answer, God sets forth the undeniable evidence: Abel's blood cries out from the ground (v. 10). It is worth noting that his life is represented by his blood and not his lifeless body or departed spirit. The author of Genesis was no Platonic dualist. The "real Abel" was not a soul floating about somewhere else but was connected to his spilled blood. Life and blood are connected all throughout Torah (e.g., Lev 17:11), including God's postdiluvian declaration of the sacredness of all life, human and animal (Gen 9:4-6).

The ground from which Abel's blood cries is more than a porous surface beneath his feet. It is a significant part of God's good creation. It, too, was deeply impacted by the negative consequences of sin. In chapter 3, it was cursed so as not to freely produce food for the ungrateful humans. Now, Cain has soiled the soil with Abel's blood. The ground cannot help but receive it. This time, God allows the earth to respond. Because Cain has defiled it in this way, the soil will no longer yield even a Fall-reduced harvest for him. The first human-born farmer must find a new occupation (v. 12).

To Cain this is more than vocational reassignment. To be barred from the soil, in his estimation, is to be barred from God's face (v. 14). Perhaps this is because Cain experienced God in his work. This is an important statement about the nature of farming, but it also points to Cain's sense of belonging where God had placed him. For God to ban him from his appointed post was for God to give up on his providential purposes for Cain, and this was the only life Cain knew. This is the first clear statement that sin somehow separates humans from God's presence. There is a sense in which all humans who distance themselves from God's good creation, whether through violence or environmental abuse, also distance themselves from God.

Cain is also deeply concerned about his personal safety. If he is to wander the earth, he will eventually encounter other humans. These humans will not want to share this world with a killer. In a well-intentioned effort to make this world a safer place for their loved ones, wider society will organize a self-righteous lynch mob to locate and terminate this murderer. How else could they feel safe? Who knows when Cain might strike again?

This societal impulse to execute killers is, perhaps, the most primitive form of the sword-bearing state.[70] So God's response is surprising—even scandalous. He sides with the guilty slayer against the presumably innocent wider citizenry. He doesn't merely forbid the killing of Cain; he vows that whoever kills Cain will face sevenfold vengeance. God's first word to a society that would organize itself into a force that would kill to protect its own security is hardly affirming. In essence, he warns, "Be careful, because if you take lethal justice into your own hands you will have to answer to me, and I am far more capable of exacting vengeance than you are."

Cain had no right to take the life of Abel. Life belongs to God. Likewise, wider society may not take Cain's life, even though he deserves it. Life is not theirs to give and take. As the story unfolds, God eventually grants authority to certain humans to take certain lives at certain times (Gen 9:5-6). But we should not read that later development back into this account. We should read later developments in light of this account, for it was written to place them in proper perspective. God reveals himself from the start as a God who wishes to limit violence and even spare the life of those who deserve death. Cain is not the only one. God doesn't shy from making extensive use of killers such as Moses (Exod 2), David (2 Sam 11-12), and Saul of Tarsus (Acts 8:1; 9:1).

Readers have long speculated what Cain's mark may be. Ruther Mellinkoff divides the most common theories into three helpful categories: marks on his body (like a cross on the forehead), a movement of his body (like groaning or

---

[70] See Yoder, "On Generating Alternative Paradigms," 58.

trembling), or a blemish upon his body (like leprosy or horns).[71] It may be, at the end of the day, that God's threat of sevenfold vengeance is itself the mark.[72] Whatever the mark, God reveals himself in this account as a God of grace. He is not boiling over with wrath that needs to be satisfied. He is moved to compassion to protect a murderer, without negating the negative consequences of his crime. Cain must still adapt to the new life he created for himself—a life of estrangement from the soil.

4:17-26 Contrasting Legacies of Cain and Seth

Cities New and Old

Cities of Antiquity
One of the other challenges for the modern reader is the temptation to read back into Genesis (or any other urban context throughout Scripture) the current realities of cities today. Based upon population alone, we might think of these cities in antiquity as merely regional "towns" compared with the megacities of today. Yet there are commonalities of cities throughout history as well as markers for what makes them healthy or unhealthy, so it is important to understand the context of these cities within Scripture, and judge where the commonalities are still present and instructive. The first city mentioned in Scripture (Enoch) may have a dubious beginning with Cain as its founder, but we see some of the exciting cultural developments within it that make cities today desirable.
Sean Benesh

---

[71] Ruth Mellinkoff, *The Mark of* Cain (Berkeley, CA: University of California Press 1981), 22-80; R. W. L. Moberly, "The Mark of Cain – Revealed at Last," *Harvard Theology Review* 100 (2007): 11-28.

[72] This position is advocated by R. W. L. Moberly, "The Mark of Cain," 11-28.

Genesis 4:17-26 is an important passage for missiology—especially urban missiology.[73] It provides an etiology (or origin account) of the city. Several factors complicate interpretation of this account. These are rooted in biases that we bring to Scripture that often exercise undue influence on our interpretation and sometimes obstruct our ability to hear God's Word to us.

People like me (having grown up in New York) cannot help but think fondly of cities. They are places of cultural diversity, architectural marvels, inspiring stage performances, niche shopping opportunities, spectacular parks, professional sporting events, and succulent ethnic and local foods. For people of considerable means who live in the suburbs and are insulated from the shadow sides of the city, urban centers serve as an exciting recreation destination.

Many who grew up in or near rundown cities—or, at least, rundown districts of cities—have a dramatically different perspective. For them, cities evoke images of cold stares, con artists, pickpockets, cultural depravity, dilapidated housing projects, sexual assault, and gang violence. They find it difficult to resonate with the well-to-do who populate the theaters, arenas, and skyscrapers.

Mission-minded Christians approach this passage from additional angles. Some see a massive conglomeration of people who need to hear and receive the gospel. Others see a wide variety of unique contexts, each of which requires indigenous incarnational churches to embrace, display, and proclaim God's kingdom. Still others see citizens from other countries who might come to know Christ and then return to their home countries and take the gospel with them. Cities are thus viewed as strategic outposts for local

---

[73] My understanding of this account has been enriched by Margaryta Teslina's award-winning paper, "City Under Siege: The Questionable Legacy of Cain and His Descendants." This paper won first place in the 2014 Stone-Campbell Journal undergraduate student paper competition.

and global Christian mission. The great potential of modern day cities has led many readers to an overly optimistic assessment of the first city recorded in Genesis. In this vein, one missiologist has said, "The city, from the beginning, was a place of refuge and community. God's command to multiply, fill the earth, and subdue it eventually point[s] to the city as a place of commerce, order, and worship."[74]

We ought to be careful, however, not to project too much of our contemporary experiences back onto Genesis 4. One way to gain some critical distance is to study the state of cities at the time and place of the originally intended audience of Genesis. This audience may have thought of major cities in their time, like Jerusalem, Damascus, Nineveh, or Ur. These would have been places of high cultural and political achievement. They were populated by kings and wealthy citizens, many of whom would have found their employment through the king.

Another way to gain critical distance is to view this account in light of other cities mentioned in Genesis. As the narrative unfolds, we encounter Babel (which God scatters for disobedience in ch. 11), Sodom and Gomorrah (which God destroys for depravity in ch. 19), a Hittite city (where Abraham is hustled in ch. 23), Haran (which has a reputation for trapping the Patriarchs in chs. 24, 29-31), and Shechem (where Jacob's daughter Dinah is raped by a prince in ch. 34).

In the historical context of ancient Israel and the literary context of Genesis, cities were neither beacons of hope nor strategic missionary posts. They were places of concentrated power where upwardly mobile people strive to make a name for themselves. While there is some continuity with cities in our own day, there is also a good deal of discontinuity. The average Israelite was not

---

[74] Scott Sunquist, *Understanding Christian Mission: Participation in Suffering and Glory* (Grand Rapids, MI: Baker Academic, 2013), 345-346.

upwardly mobile, and the nation as a whole had few impressive cities. The original audience of Genesis likely would have looked upon cities with ambivalence. For all their promise to unite and protect, they often became centers of alienation and exploitation. This is likely why Isaiah prophesied the end of both the desert wilderness and the city—to be replaced with fruitful fields, free-ranging animals, and peaceful dwelling places by streams (Isa 20:15-20). With this in mind, let us turn to Genesis 4:17-24.

Cain's Descendants Found a City (4:17-24)

> **Cities the Result of the Fall?**
>
> While the first city mentioned in Scripture has dubious beginning we certainly see the potential destructive and corruptive influence that cities can have by Genesis 11. Because of that progression we can identify this as one of the underlying reasons that Christians have denounced and renounced the city, often claiming that cities are inherently evil and the direct result of the Fall. But are they? Are cities simply the result of human rebellion or were they part of God's original blueprint from the beginning? While tainted with sin, cities are a reflection of what is both best and worst about humanity.
>
> *Sean Benesh*

Let us not forget that Cain was recently banished from the soil for shedding blood, which he (v. 14) and the author (v. 16) associated with being driven from God's presence. Indeed, God is ominously absent from the remaining story of Cain and his descendants.[75] There are no more conversations, whether for good or for ill—even when Lamech kills a man in verse 23 (as Cain did) and aspires to be like God in verse 24 (like Adam and Eve did). God is

---

[75] Wittenberg offers insightful analysis of Cain's estrangement from the soil and God's conspicuous absence from the story of his descendants ("Alienation and Emancipation," 111-13).

apparently uninvolved in the construction of the first city, as well as its internal governance.

The account moves quickly to Cain's great-great-great-grandson: Lamech. Immediately we are told that he has two wives. This is a departure from Edenic marriage. Lamech does not leave his father to cling to his wife and become one flesh with her. It appears that these two women have left their parents to join their husband who chooses to become one flesh with both of them. This means perversion insofar as these women have become one flesh with one another. It means deprivation insofar as each one must settle for less than their husband's full devotion. It fulfills God's warning that husbands will begin to rule over their wives and that their desire will be for their husbands.

Lamech also anticipates the "sons of God" in chapter 6, who take multiple women for themselves, and the kings of Egypt and Philistia, who seek to enlarge their polygamous harems by taking the wife of Abraham and almost the wife of Isaac. Of course, he also anticipates Abraham who is talked into sleeping with Sarah's maidservant and Jacob who is tricked by his father-in-law into marrying two of his daughters. In all of these scenarios, the polygamous arrangement leads to disaster. Despite popular belief, Genesis and the wider Old Testament do not endorse polygamy. They simply report it matter-of-factly when it happens. Polygamy is real and should be named for what it is. Christians today typically avoid doing so because they have embraced modern day contractual definitions of marriage. According to a biblical perspective, in which intercourse consummates a marriage, contemporary culture is replete with serial polygamy, though we cloak it in less offensive terms like pre-marital or extra-marital sex. Nonetheless, polygamy it is not approved in Scripture. It happens most often with kings, since only the wealthy could afford multiple wives. In Torah, God forbids even kings from taking multiple wives (Deut 17:17). And if they may not do it, no one may. In Genesis 4, then, Lamech is presented as a primitive king in the most primitive city.

Lamech's wives, Adah and Zillah, bear sons whose offspring pioneer three occupations associated with city life.[76] According to the NRSV translation, Jabal's descendants "live in tents and have livestock" (v. 20), Jubal's descendants "play the lyre and pipe" (v. 21), and Tubal-Cain "made all kinds of bronze and iron tools" (v. 22). This translation makes it seem as if these men are the fathers of stockbreeding, music, and the crafts. It is not hard to look at this list and see the core essentials of city life: food, entertainment, and industry. It is the beginning of civilization as we know it, and it is presumed to be good or at least morally neutral. But this translation is too simplistic, and it masks what may be a subtle critique of typical ancient Near Eastern cities.

In Hebrew, verse 20 says quite literally that Jabal is the father of "he who dwells in a tent and livestock/property." Two things stand out about this verse. First, tent dwellers typically reside outside of cities. In the Old Testament, they are contrasted with those who live in houses (Jer 35:7, thus nomadic) or who live in the field (Gen 25:27, thus away from land). Second, it is not immediately clear in what sense Jabal can be the "father" of property (the primary meaning) or livestock (the secondary meaning, to the extent that livestock indicated one's net worth). This passage is therefore difficult to translate.

Jabal's descendants may have been those who live in tents and focus on property acquisition, whether livestock or otherwise (cf. 2 Chron 14:15). This could be the beginning of suburbia, smaller villages that were close enough to cities to be counted as part of them (e.g., Num 21:25; 2 Chron 13:19). Perhaps these tent dwellers constituted a primitive merchant class of economic middlemen who profited immensely by mediating between those inside and outside the city walls. They are like those greedy men who waited outside the city gate on Sabbath eager to begin

---

[76] Lamech's daughter Naamah is not discussed at length, but her name means "charming" (v. 22).

trading (Neh 13:19-21). Such people were often the source of economic injustice and were frequently criticized by the prophets.[77]

If this passage does refer to livestock traders who lived by cities, this raises the question of what purpose their livestock served. God had not yet authorized the consumption of animals for food. He provides plants and trees to supply human food in 1:29 and doesn't authorize animal sacrifice for food until 9:3.

Tubal-Cain's trade is equally dubious. Metallurgy may be an admirable trade to modern folk, but ancient Israelites would have been deeply suspicious of metalworkers. Metal was good for three things: idols, weapons, and farming equipment. Idol-making was off-limits for Israel, as was maintaining a standing army.[78] The strong connection between metalworkers and warfare is evident in 2 Kings 24:16, where metalworkers are presumed to be capable warriors. That the Israelites were relatively unskilled smiths is evident in 1 Samuel 13:19-20 and 1 Kings 7:13-14, where they contract out such work to neighboring peoples.[79]

Farming equipment, on the other hand, was a necessity. In the context of early Genesis, however, it accentuated God's

---

[77] See Hos 12:7; Amos 8:4-6; Mic 6:10.

[78] The consistent theme of Torah is that God will fight for his people Israel. He is their military offense and defense. Torah makes provision for nearly everything the Israelites needed, except a standing army. Should they choose a king, he is expressly forbidden from acquiring horses and chariots from Egypt (Deut 17:16). When God tells Samuel to warn the Israelites about the terrible things a king will do to them, he includes recruiting their sons to fight for him and run with his horses and chariots (1 Sam 8:10-12). David is most severely punished near the end of his life for counting his fighting men (2 Sam 24).

[79] The archeological evidence supports the notion that the Israelites possessed far less iron weaponry than their neighbors. See James Muhly, "How Iron Technology Changed the Ancient World and Gave the Philistines a Military Edge," *Biblical Archaeology Review* 8, no. 6, 1982, 40-54.

curse upon the soil. It's almost as if Cain's descendants sought to overcome his estrangement from the soil by building such powerful, indestructible equipment that the soil would have to yield to their force. Metallurgy continued to be a suspect profession among Jews in the Second Temple period. First Enoch 8:1 names it a mystery that fallen angels taught humans. It enabled them to make weapons of warfare, which resulted in the earth being filled with violence, which ultimately precipitated the flood.

Two of Lamech's sons certainly occupied professions that other nations counted essential for human thriving, but not necessarily God's people. Could the same be said of Jubal? What harm could come from flautists and string pluckers? Surely music is a neutral practice. Yet, again, the Hebrew raises questions. We are told, in verse 21, that Jubal begets "those who *seize* lyre and flute." The word for "seized" is almost always a violent term. It next appears when Potiphar's wife seizes Joseph's garment as he flees from her sexual advances (Gen 39:12). It is also used in the context of raping virgins (Deut 22:28), besieging cities (Deut 20:19), capturing people (Josh 8:23), and misusing God's name (Prov 30:9). In its over sixty occurrences in Scripture, this term is never used to indicate playing music.[80]

Since this passage is routinely assumed to be detailing the happy development of high civilization as we know it today, translators simply translate it as "play," which makes these persons out to be ordinary musicians. That could be right. Elsewhere the term is used with less violent connotations (Jer 2:8, refers to those who seize Torah, but do not obey it). But what if Genesis 1-11 is not as fond of high civilization as we are? God was certainly not pleased with Babel, which anticipates the high civilization of

---

[80] The closest parallel we have to this kind of meaning are a handful of instances when the term is used in connection with handling a sword (Ezek 21:11, 30:21, 38:4). Even then, violent overtones are present.

Babylon out of which God calls Abram—or with Egypt, out of which God calls the Israelites.

Moreover, this account doesn't culminate in the glory of civilization, but in murder and escalating vengeance (Gen 4:23-24). Cain's story begins with murder and estrangement from the soil and ends with building a city and escalating murder and revenge. The same Lamech who built this city and fathered the sons who pioneered its activities kills a man and boasts about it to his wives. What is worse, he takes God's own words to limit violence and revenge against Cain and he amplifies them to his own advantage: "If Cain is avenged sevenfold, truly Lamech seventy-sevenfold." Just like ancient kings, he takes life into his own hands and he claims god-like authority for himself. In Genesis 4, Lamech's legacy is not framed as progress, but regress.

If all of this were so, then "those who seize instruments" could have negative connotations, just like tent dwellers and metalworkers. Their occupation could refer to the way in which city dwellers numb their sense of estrangement from God's good creation with the soothing sounds of music. It could also refer to the way kings of old commandeered music to serve imperial aims. Think here of Saul fetching David to sooth his tormented soul or David reducing the Levites—the once sacred guardians of blood and holy space—to court musicians. Think of Nebuchadnezzar who requires all people to bow before his symbol of national unity whenever the instruments play (Dan 3).

What was once a simple pleasure enjoyed by commoners around the fire has become a cottage industry for hire, subjugation, and idolatry. It is difficult to tell what exactly this phrase means in Genesis 4, but the ambiguity in the Hebrew should not be lost upon us. Nor should we superimpose our cultural appreciation for music, metallurgy, and merchandise back onto this narrative such that it affirms our own cultural proclivities. In fact, these narratives may have been written precisely to warn people like us!

What should we make of Genesis 4's negative account of the first city, which is later followed by Genesis 11's negative account of the first postdiluvian city? At the least, it should caution us about the city's negative potential. We ought not be enamored by the bright lights and big money. But this does not make cities any less strategic locations for Christian mission. We don't avoid cities because they're not all that they're cracked up to be. We infiltrate cities precisely because they're not all that they're cracked up to be. The more they destroy lives, the more God's people need to proclaim his offer of new life that is truly abundant. The more they numb people's senses to their estrangement from the creator and his good creation, the more we need to plant churches there that embrace, display, and proclaim God's kingdom—the new creation that has already begun in Christ.[81]

Seth's Descendants Invoke God's Name (4:25-26)

Cain's descendants merely institutionalized their estrangement from God's good creation, so God's salvation must come from somewhere else. Eve has another son, Seth (vv. 25-26). His name means "to appoint." With this name, Eve acknowledges that God has appointed her a son to replace Abel, the son who lived in greater harmony with God. Seth's descendants appear to have picked up where Abel left off. All we know is that they begin to call upon Yahweh, the personal name of Israel's God, which God later reveals to Moses on Mt. Sinai.

We are not told how they learn God's name. That is not important. What is important for God's people is to recognize that the path of Cain leads to a dead end and not a new beginning. So God's redemptive story will have to take Seth's offspring as its point of departure.

---

[81] There is a second way in which cities numb people. By overstimulating and gratifying our thirst for pleasure seeking and enjoyment, they numb our ability to find satisfaction and joy in the everyday, less glitzy gifts that God gives us.

5:1-32 Adam's Son to Noah's Sons

It is easy to ignore a genealogy. One might especially justify skipping past one in a commentary devoted to missiology. But it is precisely out of missiological concerns that we ought to slow down and listen to voices that seem strange and different from our own. Ancient genealogies are indeed strange to us. They hardly conform to modern expectations. They do not appear to be comprehensive, the numbers seem to be intentionally manipulated and, in this chapter, the ages enumerated strain credulity.[82] No less than seven men live over 900 years!

Particularly offensive to contemporary sensibilities is the exclusive nature of ancient genealogies. Though Genesis 5 begins by acknowledging that God created both male and female in his image, women go unnamed throughout the ensuing list. Furthermore, we know that Adam and Eve had other children, yet Cain and Abel's memory is nearly erased by omission from this list. All of this makes us wonder what other important figures are left out. Must history always be written by the victors?

In an insightful article, Ingeborg Löwisch draws upon Jacques Derrida and Sigmund Freud to explain some of the erasing effects of genealogies.[83] Freud applies the morbid label "death drive" to the obsession with repetition and formulaic structures that allows for absolute forgetfulness in genealogies. Such repetition reinforces an author's

---

[82] For instance, they are all multiples of 5 or multiples of 5 plus the significant number 7. This is why all the ages end in either 0, 5, 7, 2 (since 5+7 = 12) or 9 (since 5 + 7 +7 = 19). See the excellent chart in Carol A. Hill, "Making Sense of the Numbers of Genesis," *Perspectives on Science and Christian Faith: Journal of the American Scientific Affiliation* 55, no. 4 (Dec 2003), 245.

[83] Ingeborg Löwisch, "Gender and Ambiguity in the Genesis Genealogies: Tracing Absence and Subversion Through the Lens of Derrida's Archive Fever," in *Embroidered Garments: Priests and Gender in Biblical Israel*, 60-73 (Sheffield: Sheffield Phoenix Press, 2009).

agenda and, in the process, silences or destroys what lays beyond their purview. Derrida calls the genealogist's obsession with order "archive fever." This tendency appears to be at work in the *Toledoth* formula of Genesis. According to Löwisch, "The meticulous register of names and data, the careful composition of relationships and dependencies, and the commitment to a genre so different from the more exciting one of storytelling all testify to passionate archivization."[84]

Yet, on occasion, the canopy of the system is pierced, and outside light shines through the hole. Sometimes that hole is large enough to give us a substantial glimpse of what is outside. Other times it is too small to see much of anything except that there is, indeed, an outside. Still other times we capture but a fragmentary glimpse of the outside, which is enough only to spark our imaginations as to what might actually lie beyond, but not enough to convince us of precisely what we see.

All three of these scenarios play out in Genesis 5. The overriding agenda and basic literary formula are straightforward enough. As source critics have long affirmed, the genealogists appear to be of priestly background. The *Toledoth* formula that begins this genealogy continues through the rest of Genesis and finds its fulfillment in Exodus and Numbers. Exodus 6:16-27 points to the descendants of Levi, the priestly tribe, and culminates in Aaron. Numbers 3:1-4 highlights the lineage of Aaron, the most noteworthy head of Israel's priestly office. From a long-range view, then, we see that the genealogies of the Pentateuch combine (among other reasons) to legitimate the primordial legitimacy of the Aaronic priesthood.

The chosen literary formula is simple. For nearly every primeval figurehead, we are told how old they were when they had a particular son, the name of that son, how long

---

[84] Löwisch, "Gender and Ambiguity," 67.

they lived after the birth of that son, the fact that they had other sons and daughters, how many years they lived altogether, and the fact that they died. Such formulaic repetition typifies ancient genealogies. It is the sturdy framework that supports the overarching canopy. But then there are holes in the canopy or departures from the steady norm. In analyzing these holes, we see the distinct emphases of Genesis 5.

Seth

The first hole is obvious, and we encounter it right at the beginning. We are told that Seth was born in the likeness and image of Adam (5:3). Language of likeness occurs nowhere else in the genealogy, but its purpose is transparent. The genealogy begins in verses 1-2 by emphasizing that God created humankind in his likeness, both male and female. So this genealogy goes all the way back to the beginning (1:26-27). It is the record of the perpetuation of the very good human race that God originally created.

In eventually succumbing to sin, humans had not forfeited God's image. It has not been lost until the time of Abraham or Christ as some theologians suppose. The story of the Bible is *not* about the human quest to regain our lost image or the divine quest to restore it to us. Humanity as a race continues to bear God's image and function as his representatives among all of creation. We continue to exercise dominion on God's behalf, regardless of how well or poorly we do so. This fact is celebrated in Psalm 8. Furthermore, God affirms his abiding image in us immediately after the flood. He underscores the sacredness of all human lifeblood on the basis that we have been made in his image (9:6).

Cities Reflecting the Best and the Worst

While noting the abiding image of God within all of humanity despite our transgressions, this perfectly summarizes the nature of cities. They both reflect what is great about humanity as well as what is broken. In cities we

> see and experience awe-inspiring creativity and innovation, heart-moving care and concern, community, the flourishing of cultures, and more. And yet at the same time we are butted up against systemic racism, business and political corruption, apathy, isolation, oppression, and much more. Cities reflect what is best and worst about humanity and points to the theological reality that while we are made in the image of God we are tainted with sin and rebellion.
>
> *Sean Benesh*

It is also worth noting that Seth was not Adam's firstborn son. Most genealogies observe the right of primogeniture—the right of the firstborn. This often had to do with property ownership, which favored eldest sons for various reasons. It is quite likely that the rest of the sons named in this genealogy are firstborn sons, since after their birth its says in Hebrew "and *then* he bore sons and daughters." The NRSV is probably right in adding "*other* sons and daughters." The implication is that the firstborn is listed, and "then" subsequent offspring are alluded to as a group. This was standard practice in ancient genealogies. Less standard is that Seth, the third-born son, kicks off the genealogy. Yet we know that Cain was born first. The motive seems clear. Because Cain killed his brother, was estranged from the soil, and founded a city where his legacy of violence escalated alongside other questionable aspects of godless civilization, the pure priestly line must run through another son of Adam, namely, Seth. This particular hole in the canopy therefore allows readers to see how God identifies key people who will play important roles in his saving mission.

New Beginnings

In the person of Seth, a new beginning was established even though he was the third born son of Adam and Eve. Cain killed Abel and founded a city and legacy that was marked by violence. Seth was a clean break from this trajectory. Throughout history God continues to call out key people like Seth for a new beginning. Applied to the

> city we can look at key figures who affected the city for good throughout history. This ranges from urban planners to politicians to activists and the like. How can you be a change agent in your city?
>
> *Sean Benesh*

Enoch

After Seth's genealogical divergence, the normal pattern continues until the seventh generation: Enoch. Here the hole in the canopy is not so big and the meaning of the divergence not so clear. After Enoch bears his son Methuselah, we are told twice that he "walked with God" and, after living for 365 years, "was no more, because God took him" (v. 24). Enoch is thus the only man whose death is not mentioned using the typical formula: "and he died." Perhaps God taking him means that he did die, just not a natural death. Because he walked with God, he was not allowed to experience a protracted painful end. God simply put him to rest peacefully. This sort of ending is like that of Moses, who died in peak health at the perfect age of 120 (a multiple of 12 and 10), but whose burial place is unknown because God buried him (Deut 34:5-7).

Or, perhaps Enoch's departure paralleled that of Elijah who didn't experience a normal death, but was taken by God into the heavens (or sky) by way of a fiery chariot (2 Kgs 2:11). Where the chariot landed, nobody knows. Malachi 4:5 expects Elijah to return at a later time to prepare for the day of the LORD. Yet Jesus states that "no one has ascended into heaven except the one who descended from heaven, the Son of Man" (John 3:13).

There appears to be some sort of backstory to Enoch's departure to which we are not privy. Philip Davies argues that the missing account is the same tradition that stands behind the book of 1 Enoch, which depicts Enoch as being taken into heaven to learn secrets from God about how erring angels taught humans all sorts of evil, which led to the rampant wickedness that precipitated the flood.[85]

Interestingly, the community behind 1 Enoch placed great importance on the solar calendar with a 364-day year (1 Enoch 82:6) as opposed to the lunar calendar of 360 days. This is interesting because God "took" Enoch at the age of 365. Still, this theory relies on some questionable presuppositions that we will examine in connection with Genesis 6:1-4. Nonetheless, this brief discussion of Enoch testifies to a genealogy that is rich in texture, even when we cannot fully grasp its full fabric.

Noah

Safety in the City
We are reminded that in ancient times, military might in the form of weaponry or walls was one of the most notable features of cities. This notion of protection and projection of military might finds its way into the narrative of our cities today. While cities today are not surrounded by high walls we turn to the same question, "Are the people in the city safe?" However, that question more than ever leads us into broader conversations about affordable housing, access to jobs, marginalized people, neighborhood safety, immigration reform, and so much more. **Are people in our cities today safe?**
Sean Benesh

The genealogical account of Noah differs from the rest of the genealogy in ways that are both transparent and opaque. The author breaks formula by indicating that Lamech introduces his son Noah as the one who, from out of the cursed ground (*adamah*), will bring humanity relief from our work (5:29). This appears to be a reference to the fact that Noah is later described as a man of the soil (*adamah*) who plants a vineyard that produces wine (9:20-21). In the ancient world, alcohol was considered a great

---

[85] Philip R. Davies, "And Enoch Was Not, For Genesis Took Him," in *Biblical Traditions in Transmission: Essays in Honour of Michael A. Knibb* (Leiden: Brill, 2006), 97-107.

blessing for humans, despite their tendency to abuse it. We see this also in the Epic of Gilgamesh's account of the creation of ale.⁸⁶

The other element that stands out in the account of Noah is not so much a break from form as a break from expectations. Before his time, the average age when men bore their first son was 117. They started as young as 65 and as old as 187. After Noah, the average drops to 50, with a range from 29 to 100. It therefore sticks out like a sore thumb that Noah did not bear his three sons until the age of 500 (5:32). Surely this means something, but the text gives no clues. The surrounding context does, however, provide modest grounds for speculation. We might take some guidance from what it says positively about Noah and negatively about wider society.

Like Enoch, we are later told that Noah "walked with God" (6:9). He was a righteous man who was blameless in his generation. This begs the question, What brought about his generation's guilt? We are told that they were violent and wicked (6:11-13). But what exactly does that mean? The violence of Noah's generation did not arise in a vacuum; it takes place within the unfolding story of Genesis. God created Adam and Eve to be perfect counterparts. The man was called to leave his parents' household and cling to his wife. After humans sinned, Adam began ruling over his equal partner, Cain killed Abel, and Lamech made two women cling to him while killing a man and escalating the threat of vengeance beyond divine proportions. Cain then builds a city where men are estranged from the soil and begin developing the technology behind advanced weaponry. Next we hear about the "sons of God" taking a plurality of wives for themselves and the rise of a warrior class upon the earth. All of this leads up to Noah's wicked generation.

---

⁸⁶ Robert S. Kawashima, "*Homer Faber* in J's Primeval History," *Zeitschrift fur die alttestamentliche Wissenschaft* 116, no. 4 (2004): 483-501.

Two themes stand out in humanity's gradual descent into depravity. First, men exchange God's monogamous, mutually loving design for marriage with spousal subjugation and neglect through polygamy. Second, humans exchange peaceful coexistence with one another for violence, vengeance, and death. We already noted that Noah was a man of the soil (9:20), so it is quite likely that he avoided the growing violence of city life. Perhaps his late-in-life fathering testifies to his radical faithfulness to his marriage covenant.

Bearing children was vital to survival in Noah's day. The fact that he had no children until 500 strongly suggests that his wife was barren (like Sarah, Rebekah, and Rachel). Had Noah sought to secure his future the way most men did, his most viable option was to have intercourse with and thus marry another woman. Yet out of faithfulness to his wife and trust in God's provision, he apparently did not. This means that one of two things happened. Either God rewarded his faithfulness by opening his wife's womb at a late age or he waited until his wife died. Then only after death dissolves his marital covenant does he marry another woman who is able to conceive. Either way, this odd number quite possibly constitutes a subtle link between Noah's uncommon righteousness and his late-in-life fatherhood.[87]

Repeated Death

If one way to hear the "other" voice in this genealogy is to interpret it on its own terms and observe how it breaks form with its own conventions, another way is to interpret it in the wider context of the Genesis narrative.

Genesis 5 is not the only genealogy. There are other genealogies in Genesis, and certainly other genealogies throughout Scripture. Yet this one stands out from them all in one important regard: each entry, except for Enoch's,

---

[87] Malachi 2:10-16 also makes a strong connection between faithfulness to God and faithfulness to one's spouse.

ends by indicating that the ancient figure died. Of course, it is implied in all genealogies that each person listed eventually died. But why end each entry with the morbid phrase, "and then he died"? The answer goes back to Genesis 2. When God placed Adam in the garden of Eden, he warned him not to eat of the tree of knowledge lest he die. In chapter 3, the serpent raised the possibility that the humans may eat from it without dying. This was a risk that the humans were willing to take. To the surprise of first time readers, Adam and Eve did not die. The serpent appeared to be correct. The humans gained God-like knowledge and continued to live. They continued to live so much so that God drove them out of the garden so they would no longer access the tree of life and, in so doing, live forever.

With the murder of Abel and the victim of Lamech, we learn quickly that death was a reality. But perhaps they were exceptions—the sorry fate of unfortunate humans who crossed the wrong person in the wrong way and were killed in cold blood. Could it be that all other humans would continue living? Not according to Genesis 5. This genealogy makes clear with each chilling final refrain that *all* humans die, not just the unlucky ones. With its morbid drumbeat cadence, this chapter may fittingly be called the genealogy of death.

Long Life

When we compare Genesis 5 with other genealogies, we also note that humans tend to live excessively long lives. Scholars have surmised a wide array of theories to account for this phenomenon. Carol Hill skillfully lists those views, critiques them, and suggests why we are better off understanding long lifespans as a literary convention of their time and not as a strictly mathematical statement of how long people actually lived.[88] In fact, she sternly warns that to read these numbers literally is itself a mythological

---

[88] Hill, "Making Sense of the Numbers," 239-251.

project that does not proceed from faith since the original authors inflated those numbers intentionally precisely to express their faith. To make them into something that the authors did not intend is tantamount to stripping them of their religious significance altogether.[89]

Hill's argument is highly informative on multiple levels, especially regarding the shape and development of ancient numerology. But she makes little effort to interpret the ages in this chapter in light of the wider missional story that the entire primeval history tells. Though she notes, quite importantly, that God limits human lifespans to 120 in Genesis 6:3, she interprets this more as an Israelite shift away from ancient Mesopotamian sexagesimal counting systems to later Palestinian (and Egyptian) figural and decimal counting systems. While there is clearly evidence for this sort of shift, it barely scratches the surface of how a decrease in lifespans might serve God's wider saving purposes for his creation.

A fuller explanation for why God would limit lifespans must wait for our discussion of Genesis 6, but at this point we might at least make one observation about the social and political effect of long lifespans. Recall how we interpreted God driving humans away from the tree of life in Genesis 3 as an act of grace. To live forever in a state of sin would eventually lead to a life of torture. So God releases humans from lives riddled with sin's negative consequences, steadily compounding over time. He graciously gives them death or, at least, he allows them to choose death by choosing sin.

We then noticed that with the onset of sin came escalating human domination: first the man over the woman, then brother over brother, then another man over multiple women and a man whom he kills. The city Cain builds becomes a dangerous place of escalating vengeance, and powerful men begin cornering the market on societal fear

---

[89] Hill, "Making Sense of the Numbers," 250.

and power. Suppose Lamech makes good on his threat. Suppose he learns of others who plan to take his life, and then he avenges them seventy times sevenfold. Now suppose Lamech encounters another powerful man like himself and they rub each other the wrong way. A feud begins, wars ensue, camps form, and the earth becomes a battle zone with the blood of countless Abels crying out from the soil.

Modern human history has seen what a wicked ruler can accomplish in only decades of power. Now imagine someone like Hitler living 900 plus years! Long life seems great when good people are the only ones living but, as we will see in chapter 6, righteous people who walk with God are the exception, not the norm.

6:1-4 Sons of God

Classic Options

The relevance of this passage has a lot to do with how one identifies the main characters: the sons of God, the daughters of men, and the Nephilim. Trying to identify these characters has been a perennial challenge for Bible interpreters and has led to various competing theories over the centuries. Here are four of the most common theories:

	Sons of God	**Daughters of Men**	**Nephilim**
1	Angels/junior gods	Humans	Hybrids
2	Posers as demigods	Ordinary Humans	Posers claiming to be fallen gods
3	Seth's Holy/Chosen Line	Cain's Unholy/Unchosen Line	Hybrids
4	Nobility	Commoners	Giant men

Most commentators review these theories, cite the pros and cons of each one, acknowledge that we cannot be sure, and explain why they prefer some options over the others.[90]

The angels interpretation has going for it that the phrase "sons of God" means angels elsewhere in Scripture (Job 1:6), a wide sampling of Second Temple Jewish literature appears to espouse this theory (1 Enoch, Jubilees, LXX), and several New Testament books appear to endorse it (Jude 6; 1 Pet 3:19-20; 2 Pet 2:4). Against this theory is that humans are punished and not angels. It is also doubtful that humans and angels could procreate together for biblical (Mark 12:24-25) and physiological reasons.

That the sons of God might be junior gods has significant parallels in mythological literature surrounding Israel, and it would certainly explain why their hybrid offspring would be impressive warriors. Its primary weakness is that Genesis appears to intentionally demythologize the Israelite worldview in chapter 1 and, even though the earliest generations of Israelites had to be weaned off polytheistic sensibilities, there is good reason to believe that the original canonical audience of Genesis was predominantly monotheistic by then.

A variant of this view is that this account depicts humans who were claiming to be "sons of God" on grounds that they were uniquely endowed with extraordinary size and strength. They merely posed as "fallen ones" (the root meaning of *Nephilim*) insofar as they pretended to be demigods that had fallen from the heavens. This view transcends some of the limits of the above views, but 6:1-4 altogether lacks language suggesting pretense. We are not told that anyone is deceiving anyone else.

The theory of the godly and ungodly competing lines of Seth and Cain has in its favor that Genesis pits them against each other in chapters 4-5. It is also important later in Genesis that God's chosen people not intermarry with foreigners (Gen 28:1). However, it is unclear how mixing chosen righteous people with unchosen unrighteous people would produce extraordinary individuals like the Nephilim.

---

[90] For helpful reviews see Hamilton, *The Book of Genesis*, 261-272; Kissling, *Genesis*, vol. 1, 259-269.

Further, it seems a bit early in the story to assert a strong distinction between these two lines since both are washed away in the flood and only one family from the line of Seth endures.

The royal versus commoner theory has in its favor that some royalty in the ancient Near East certainly spoke of themselves in divine terms. Pharaoh of Egypt presented himself as a divine son, and Israel's own kings were spoken of in similar language (2 Sam 7:14; Ps 2:7). Pagan and Israelite nobility were also notorious for taking commoner women for themselves (Gen 12:15; 20:2; 2 Sam 11). The most frequently cited problem with this theory is that kings are nowhere in Scripture—whether individually or collectively—referred to as "sons of God."

More Recent Conversations

Over the last fifteen years, scholars have refined the above views and introduced new alternatives. They have breathed fresh air into a debate that appeared to have grown stale. After reviewing five proposals, I set forth my own preferred interpretation.

1. Competing Traditions

According to Philip Davies this passage is ancient folklore that presupposes a wider mythological framework to which we no longer have direct access.[91] Making extensive use of source criticism, he argues that the Priestly author of 6:1-4 operated with an account of sin's origins quite different from what we see in chapters 3-4. Davies suggests that the Genesis 6 account is based on the same ancient tradition upon which 1 Enoch depends. First Enoch thus provides our closest extant access to it. In the Enochian tradition, rebellious angels descended from heaven, taught humans all the wicked elements of civilization (including music and metallurgy), procreated with human women to spawn a race of angel-human hybrids that dominated the masses,

---

[91] Davies, "And Enoch Was Not," 97-107.

and filled the earth with the wickedness and violence that necessitated the flood.

The Yahwist author, who is presumed to have written Genesis 2-4, rejected this tradition and sought to replace it with a rival account. According to that account, humans aspired to be like God by eating forbidden fruit, God separated them from the tree of life so they would die, and after further estranging themselves from God and soil they eventually built a city where they developed the basic rudiments of fallen civilization (music and metallurgy). This is what filled the earth with such wickedness and violence that God chose to flood it. Fortunately for us, the Yahwist source did not entirely eclipse the Priestly tradition, since a fragment of their story remains in 6:1-4.

2. Blameworthy Humans

Unlike Davies, Robin Routledge seeks to strengthen the angel interpretation without driving a wedge between it and Genesis 3.[92] He seeks to overcome the greatest challenge facing the angelic interpretation: why God punishes humans and not angels when humans appear to be mere victims of angelic predation. He observes that 6:1-4 parallels 3:5-6 and 11:4 insofar as humans strive to cross boundaries between them and God in all three passages. In chapter 11, they try to build a tower that reaches into the heavens. In chapter 3, they try to become like God in knowledge. As a result, humans lose access to the tree of life and experience death. Routledge also notes strong verbal parallels in the Hebrew language of chapters 3 and 6. Just like Eve "saw" the fruit to be "good" and "took" it, the sons of God "saw" the daughters of men to be "good" and "took" them.

Routledge surmises, then, that the human motive for reproducing with angels was to achieve the immortality they lost in chapter 3. If they can mate with immortal

---

[92] Robin L. Routledge, "'My spirit' in Genesis 1-4," *Journal of Pentecostal Theology* 20, no. 2 (2011): 232-251.

beings, their offspring will possess the immortal spirit. This refusal to accept their God-mandated mortality is a punishable offense that justifies the flood.[93]

It is not clear that Routledge succeeds in strengthening the angelic interpretation. The parallel to chapter 11 is weak in as much as their building project does not attempt to cross some sort of threshold into the divine sphere. "The heavens" also means, simply, the space above the clouds. We are not told that they were trying to reach God in heaven, but they were trying to make a name for themselves on earth and trying to prevent themselves from being scattered (11:4). Also, whereas there is a strong verbal connection between 3:6 and 6:2, it is the angels in chapter 6 who "saw" humans as "good" and "took" them—not vice versa. So, if anything, this is an account of angels stooping to act like humans, not humans aspiring to be like angels. Of their own accord, humans only multiply and bear daughters (v. 1). Angels take all the boundary-crossing initiative and, still, they are not punished, nor their quasi-immortal offspring.

3. Spiritual Humans

Helge Kvanvig makes an interesting argument that approximates Routledge's thesis.[94] For him, the central question remains whether or not humans can be immortal. However, he draws most of his inspiration from the Atrahasis flood account. In it, humans were created

---

[93] Interestingly, Routledge does not believe that the withdrawal of God's spirit from humans in 6:3 has to do with the age by which humans must die ("My Spirit," 246-249). He distinguishes between the "spirit of life" that keeps us alive and the "spirit of God" that hovered over the chaotic waters in 1:2. He argues that in 120 years God will withdraw his Spirit from creation such that the chaotic waters will once again overtake the earth in the flood. Though he agrees this will result in people losing the "spirit of life," he does not believe that is what 6:3 means.

[94] Helge S. Kvanvig, "Gen 6, 1-4 as an Antediluvian Event," *Scandinavian Journal of the Old Testament* 16, no. 1 (2002): 79-112.

immortal and their multiplication became a noisy problem for the gods. The gods' solution was twofold: flood the earth and re-create humans as mortal. Similarly, Genesis 6 begins with the multiplication of humans (v. 1), follows with a statement that God will not let them live forever (v. 3), and culminates with God's resolve to rid the earth of humans through a flood (vv. 7, 13, 17).

These parallels are too strong for Kvanvig to ignore, and he finds grounds for linking the two stories in 6:3. As he reads it, there were two kinds of humans prior to the flood. There was the purely human line, which descended from *adam* who was created in Genesis 2. They came from the ground, are mortal, and had potential to live forever from the tree of life. But they were banished from it and so they die. There was also another human line according to Kvanvig: the sons of God. They were made from the spirit of God and their creation is presupposed in 6:3, which speaks of humans who possess God's immortal spirit and may thus live forever.

When these sons of God (immortal humans) began interbreeding with the daughters of *adam* (mortal humans), they begat giants who live forever and tyrannize the earth. So God puts an end to the chaos by limiting *all* human life to 120 years and sending the flood. Only the descendants of Noah survive in the ark. Since he was a descendant of Adam through Shem, only mortal humans remain after the flood. The Genesis solution to the problem of multiplying humans is the same as the Atrahasis epic, only in reverse order: God removes his spirit from humans, which denies their immortality, and then he floods the earth in such a way that only mortals remain.

4. Neanderthals

Shupert Spero also theorizes that 6:1-4 deals with the interbreeding of two fundamentally different types of human.[95] He posits that the "sons of God" are *homo*

---

[95] Shubert Spero, "Sons of God, Daughters of Men?" *Jewish Bible*

sapiens, which are the humans God created in Genesis 1-2. They appear in the fossil record around 100,000 years ago. The daughters of men, on the other hand, are *homo erectus* or Neanderthals. Scientists place them on the earth beginning around 1.5 million years ago.

It was once thought that the former evolved out of the latter, but that has recently been falsified.[96] Nonetheless, they peacefully co-existed for a while. Genesis 6 tells the story of how these two, formerly independent human societies eventually came together. *Homo Sapiens*, who were smarter and more sophisticated, began abducting female Neanderthals and mating with them. This resulted in a breed of super-sized and super-smart humans who terrorized and tyrannized others.

5. Males and Females

Elihu Schatz sets forth the most simplistic interpretation.[97] The "sons of God" are males and the "daughters of men" are females. Genesis 6 calls them this because the first male was made directly by God and the first female was made out of the first man. Thus, males are "of God" and female are "of men." Schatz's brief article gives no account of the Nephilim.

Evaluating the Alternatives

Recent theories have cracked open the old debate by raising new possibilities and highlighting key resources that help us substantiate older theories. Davies makes excellent use of source criticism and the history of interpretation. Routledge employs careful literary analysis by interpreting 6:1-4 in light of the chapters that precede and succeed it. Kvanvig offers comparative literary analysis

---

Quarterly 40, no. 1 (Jan-Mar 2012): 15-18.

[96] Spero, "Sons of God," 17.

[97] Elihu A. Schatz, "Sons of Elokim as used in Genesis," *Jewish Bible Quarterly* 36, no. 2 (Apr-June 2008): 125-26.

by making extensive use of the Athrahasis epic. Spero leverages archeological findings, and Schatz wields Ockham's Razor, figuratively speaking, to identify what is perhaps the simplest explanation.

All such tools play an important part. As noted in the introduction, however, this commentary places greater emphasis on the final form of the text and how it helps us understand the role of God's people in God's mission. Whatever original sources the final author may have employed and whatever meaning those snippets had prior to being incorporated into Genesis, the text comes to us as a carefully crafted work in which each passage is strategically and artfully woven into a wider narrative tapestry. So we are most concerned with each passage's meaning in the narrative world of Genesis and the wider canonical narrative of which Genesis is a part.

From this perspective, we see that the final author/editor, in the first eleven chapters, is culling and reorganizing Israel and wider society's ancient traditions in such a way as to set up the kinds of issues that Abraham's descendants later face.

- Chapter 1 presents creation in an orderly yet polemical fashion to help later Israelites process the competing worldviews they encounter among various nations and to introduce them to the unique Sabbath way of life to which God uniquely calls them.

- Chapter 2 illuminates their understanding of the specific role humans play in the world as well as the institution of marriage, which is critical not only to human procreation and societal organization, but also to the transmission of Israelite faith from one generation to the next.

- Chapter 3 shows how renouncing the limitations God places upon human dominion leads to friction and fragmentation in all things, which God seeks to counteract by later forming a set apart people whose Torah-formed way of life displays God's original intention of freedom and blessing within limitations.

- Chapter 4 provides an origin account for fallen visions of civilization, out of which God calls Abraham's descendants in order to make them a contrast civilization that embodies God's design for human thriving.
- The end of chapter 4 and the entirety of chapter 5 anticipate God's "contrast civilization" by foregrounding the alternative line of Seth, which culminates in Noah whose son Shem is the great ancestor of Abraham.

It makes sense, then, that chapter 6 would pick up where Cain's narrative left off. Fallen human civilization progressively gets worse—so much so that the most loving thing God can do is purge the earth of human iniquity and begin anew. Then, after the flood, certain segments of human civilization revert to the fallen trajectory of Cain and need, once again, to be redirected. Then God reaches back to the lineage of Seth, through Noah and Shem, to find another righteous ancestor to pave God's constructive way forward, namely, Abraham.

Everything in Genesis 1-11 sets the stage for everything that God later does with Abraham and his descendants. It all serves as the preface to Israel's story and the lens through which the Israelites should interpret their experiences. We should therefore expect 6:1-4, like the rest of Israel's backstory, to somehow connect to Israel's later calling and complex history—especially as told in Genesis 12-50.

The most significant shortcoming of the angel interpretation is that it seems so poorly connected to the rest of the Genesis narrative. Not only do angels go entirely unpunished in the narrative we have, but nowhere in the ensuing narrative do humans and angels interact independently of God's initiative. Angels only serve as messengers from God. They appear to have no voice or will independent from God. There is no hint that humans might fraternize with angels, let alone fornicate with them. Likewise, there are no laws in Torah that broach the subject of appropriate and inappropriate relations with angels. That being the case, we would then have a short story in a stage-setting portion of Genesis that fails to set the stage for anything significant in Israel's later legacy, self-understanding, and mission.

Something similar may be said of theories that make the human quest for immortality the central theme of 6:1-4. This theory at least has in its favor that Genesis 2-3 raises the possibility that humans might live forever. But that possibility finds its resolution and termination with expulsion from Eden in chapter 3, when humans are separated from the tree of life. After that, however, the theme disappears altogether. Nowhere in Genesis (or the rest of the Old Testament) do humans strive to achieve immortality through illicit means. The Israelites expected to die eventually and go to Sheol. No one strives to channel evil powers to emulate Enoch or Elijah. Whatever may have happened to them, we never see Israelites trying to reproduce their unusual departures from life. In Daniel 12:2, we see clear expectation of a resurrection from the dead to everlasting life or contempt. But no prophet scathes God's people for scheming or striving to live forever. Like fornicating with angels, it is simply not a temptation they faced.

The Neanderthal theory is creative, but anachronistic. Only recently did humans discover the possibility of two distinct human races. Spero provides no corroborating evidence that ancient folk were aware of a primitive, less evolved form of human. Though the Old Testament affirms the existence of giant humans, these are never identified as intellectually inferior. Furthermore, if the flood wiped them out, why do Nephilim roam the earth later on (6:4; cf. Num 13:33)? Though Schatz's theory is creative in its simplicity, it seems incomplete.

Warlords, Women, Warriors

Is there, then, a theory that accounts for all the data, fits naturally within the narrative context that proceeds and succeeds it, engages issues that would have been relevant to ancient Israelites, and somehow prepares readers for the unique mission of Abraham and his descendants? The nobility theory appears to be the most promising, but language of kingship or royalty seems a bit more sophisticated than primeval society appears to have been. It may be better to think of the "sons of God" as warlords. They are, in primitive form, what kingship will later be. Consider the supporting evidence:

- In the ancient Near East, commoners had to worry about their women being taken from them by kings. As previously noted, Abraham worried about both Pharaoh of Egypt and Abimelech of Philistia taking Sarah.[98] The laws of Torah warn any future Israelite king not to take multiple wives for himself (Deut 17:17). The previous narrative portion of Genesis presents Lamech as a primitive ruler who took multiple wives for himself. The subjugation of females to males who "rule over" them is a theme that springs directly from the Fall account of Genesis 3.

- Ancient kings also surrounded themselves with giant warriors who helped establish and maintain their reigns. The Philistines had Goliath who was famously tall (1 Sam 17), and King David surrounded himself with warriors (1 Chron 11-12). This maintains a strong connection between 6:1-3 and 6:4 and helps explain how the earth became filled with violence. There wasn't just one "son of God" taking daughters of men. There were multiple warlords building mini-armies, pillaging commoners, and vying for control of land. It is only a matter of time before these warlords encounter one another and battle for control of the same land. War and violence follow, and commoners suffer as collateral damage.

- This problem would be compounded considerably if warlords were living extremely long lives as the

---

[98] The same Hebrew word for "take" is used in each of these instances: Gen 6:2, 12:15, and 20:20. Genesis 6:2 and 12:15 also include the same word for "see."

genealogy of chapter 5 testifies. Long lives mean long reigns, which mean more control over more territory and more opportunity to clash with neighboring clans. Limiting the lifespan of humans to 120, which God appears to do in 6:3, would thus go a long way to curtail the amount of power one warlord could accrue, the number of wives he could use and abuse, and the degree of damage he could inflict upon the masses. It is also possible that 120 does not refer to the age by which most people die. It might refer to the amount of time before the flood begins and nearly everyone drowns.[99]

- This interpretation maintains a strong connection not only to Lamech's violence and wives and the long lives of chapter 5, but also with the genealogy of chapter 10 and the Babel account of chapter 11. In 10:8, Nimrod is introduced as a "mighty warrior." This is the same word used to describe the Nephilim in 6:4. We know that Nimrod used his might to take control of many territories. We are specifically told that he founded the cities of Nineveh and Babel. Nineveh is notoriously violent as the prophecy of Nahum testifies (Nah 3:19). Babel is, of course, the famous city denounced in Genesis 11—a city remembered for trying to make a "name" for itself. The word for name in 11:4 is the same word used to describe the Nephilim in 6:4. They were mighty men "of name." We will discuss this more later, but let it suffice to say that there is a strong connection between what the "sons of God" were doing with the assistance of the Nephilim in chapter 6 and what Nimrod and his city does in chapters 10-11.

- The strongest argument against this interpretation is that the term "sons of God" is never used of kings in the Old Testament. This argument is not as strong as it appears. Though those Hebrew words do not appear together in that particular order, Israelites refer to kings as God's sons in several places (e.g., 2 Sam 7:14;

---

[99] Routledge, "My Spirit," 246-249.

Ps 2:7). Moreover, in the New Testament, Jesus is referred to as the "son of God" numerous times and, in most of them, it is clear that he meant the "king" that Israel has been waiting for. For instance, in John 1:49, Nathaniel says to Jesus, "Rabbi, you are the Son of God! You are the King of Israel!" Nonetheless it is true that this was not Israel's preferred way to refer to their kings.

- One of the main reasons for this, perhaps, is that pagan kings often claimed a unique relationship to their deities. Yet this is arguably irrelevant because Genesis 6 is not referring to Israel's kings but the primeval predecessors to pagan kings! It therefore matters more that pagan kings referred to themselves in this way than it does that Israelites would refer to kings in this way. This theory may be connected to the "poser" theory listed above. "Sons of God" could be warlords who pretended to be divine offspring to legitimate their unique right to exercise dominion. Yet one of the themes we noted in Genesis 1 is that God created all humans in his image and gave all of humanity dominion. This is a subtle critique of pagan kings' false claims to privileged connections with God.

- Finally, the warlord interpretation appears to have against it that the Enochian tradition overtly identifies the "sons of God" with angels. This is the earliest extant Jewish interpretation, and the New Testament appears to endorse it in several places (Jude 6, 1 Peter 3:19-20, and 2 Peter 2:4). Yet people who make this argument seldom acknowledge that 1 Enoch is an apocalypse and that in such literature, just like in Daniel and Revelation, superhuman figures symbolically represent ordinary human figures. Furthermore, in the Old Testament, several passages make a strong connection between angels and kings (Isa 24:21-23; Ps 82:1-8; Dan 10:10-14, 18-21). This connection is grounded in the Jewish belief that God rules over all the nations by way of angels who stand over kings who reign over the people. Kings and angels therefore participate in the same chain of command that stretches between ordinary citizens and God.

It is quite likely, then, that the angelic "sons of God" in 1 Enoch symbolically represent Greek kings, the daughters of men represent the vulnerable Jewish people, and the Nephilim represent compromised Jews who embraced the Greek way of life so as to receive power and influence from Greek rulers. The judgment that God metes out to these angels and their offspring in 1 Enoch therefore instills hope in God's faithful that he will indeed judge these powerful Greek rulers and their Jewish allies in his good timing.

This explanation is supported by the fact that the Enochian tradition itself explicitly links God's judgment on disobedient angels with his judgment upon human kings and rulers (1 Enoch 63:1-64:1; 67:4-12). It is therefore quite possible that the Enochian tradition associates the "sons of God" of Genesis 6 with angels precisely because angels and kings are conceptually linked. Angels serve as the perfect symbolic superhuman counterpart to human kings.[100] To interpret 1 Enoch's symbolic portrayal of Genesis 6 literally is therefore analogous to lobbying for the literal existence of a ten-horned beast and seven-headed dragon on the basis of Daniel 7 and Revelation 12. Far from undermining the warlord interpretation of Genesis 6:1-4, the Enochian tradition, properly interpreted, actually supports it.

The warlords, women, and warriors view thus accounts for all the evidence without straining credulity. This power struggle threatened primeval society, ancient Israel, the early church, and the world in which we fulfill our role in God's mission today. Nowadays, warlords and warriors

---

[100] It is also interesting that, in the Animal Apocalypse of 1 Enoch, stars represent the sons of God. In Isaiah 14:4, 12, a star represents the king of Babylon. See also Num 24:17; Judg 5:19-20; Dan 8:10.

exude an aura of greater civility, but the havoc they wreak upon the daughters and sons of men is no less brutal.

FLOOD AND AFTERMATH 6:5—11:32

Flood: 6:5—8:19

> **Divine Disapproval**
>
> This conversation sets the stage for how we view cities and in particular how we assume that God views cities. The tensions raised in this section as we wrestle with the implications of the flood show up again in God's relationship with certain cities. For many, along with the outcome of Cain's first city, this sets the stage for God's disapproval for cities in general and certainly specific ones that are mentioned by name. However, like the account of the flood, this is much more of a nuanced conversation where we need to investigate more deeply.
>
> *Sean Benesh*

The Genesis flood seldom comes up in missiological conversations and understandably so. It appears to fly in the face of the basic impulse of Christian mission. For God so loved the world he sent Jesus to save everyone (John 3:16) is replaced with for God so rued the world he sent a flood to destroy almost everyone (Gen 6:6). Missiological interpretations of this account tend to emphasize the covenant God makes with Noah after the flood or the fact that God doesn't give up on creation even when he deems it ripe for judgment.[101] Recent biblical scholarships has focused most on three dimensions of the flood account: historical, ecological, and theological. Basic familiarity with these issues will prepare us for a careful contextual reading of this passage.

The Flood and History

In recent years, scholars have furthered twentieth century conversations about the relationship between the biblical

---

[101] See Bartholomew and Goheen, *The Drama of Scripture*, 49-51; Wright, *The Mission of God*, 326-27.

flood and scientific, archeological, and ancient literary records. Paul Seely, for instance, offers a thorough evaluation of the historical evidence for a global flood and concludes that, while it should not be taken as "VCR History," neither should it be regarded as pure fiction. Instead, he argues, "The biblical account is divinely accommodated to and integrally intertwined with the science of the times, and that accommodation to outdated science prevents it from ever being completely harmonized with modern science."[102] This ought not be considered a problem, according to Seely, because the flood story isn't told to communicate history but theology.

J. David Pleins offers a full-length monograph treatment that brings scientific and archeological concerns into conversation with ancient mythology.[103] He divides interpreters of the flood account into four camps. *Literalists* focus on the details of the text and strive to demonstrate the congruity of such details with geological and other records. *Loose literalists* affirm a looser connection to history and strive to reconstruct the actual events behind the text. *Secularizing mythologists* chalk the account up to mere mythology and exhibit a suspicious disposition toward the Genesis flood. A fourth view also associates the flood with ancient mythology, but without the negative connotations. Though Pleins doesn't label this group, one might call them *charitable mythologists*. For them, mythology is a powerful genre that conveys deep truths and meaning and should not be looked down upon for its weaker connection to history.[104] Pleins sees value in

---

[102] Paul H. Seely, "Noah's Flood: Its Date, Extent, and Divine Accommodation," *Westminster Theological Journal* 66 (2004), 311.

[103] J. David Pleins, *When the Great Abyss Opened: Classic and Contemporary Readings of Noah's Flood* (New York: Oxford University Press, 2003).

[104] For a discussion of other ancient Near Eastern flood accounts see Pleins, *When the Great Abyss Opened*, chs. 6-7.

all four camps and argues that we need to appropriate the best of each one.[105] Nonetheless, he appears to resonate most with the charitable mythology camp.

It is not clear that missiological appropriation of Genesis should be limited to the insights of any single camp. We often learn the most from those whose fundamental assumptions are quite different from our own. The ability to listen charitably to the voice of others is invaluable to an incarnational approach to mission—an approach that enters into the world of those you are trying to reach without being absorbed entirely by it.

The Flood and Ecology

Ecological interpretations have also factored prominently in recent scholarship. Steward Herman leverages the flood account to challenge readers to take climate change seriously.[106] Though God promises never to destroy humanity again by way of a flood, this doesn't mean that we humans won't destroy ourselves by neglecting the natural constraints of this world. He therefore encourages readers to learn from God's own forbearance with creation and to responsibly exercise the authority God has given us in creation.

Glenn Kreider interprets the flood with reference to wider Scriptural teachings on the future of creation (e.g., Rom 8; 2 Pet 3; Rev 20-21).[107] Since God has promised not to flood the earth again, we ought to be diligent stewards of this world. He rejects the interpretation that God only

---

[105] Pleins, *When the Great Abyss Opened*, 183-84.

[106] Steward W. Herman, "On Primal Fear and Confidence: Reinterpreting the Myth of the Flood as the Climate Changes," *Word & World* 29, no. 1 (Winter 2009): 63-74.

[107] Glenn R. Kreider, "The Flood is as Bad as It Gets: Never Again Will God Destroy the Earth," *Bibliotheca Sacra* 171 (Oct-Dec 2014): 418-439.

promised never to destroy the earth *with a flood* and that he still reserves the right to destroy it by some other means, like fire. In Kreider's view, this would undermine the hopeful image of the rainbow. Rather than assure all living creatures that God will never destroy the earth again, it would serve as a perpetual reminder that God will someday destroy the earth some other way. It thus looms over the horizon as an ominous threat and not a hope-filled promise. Such a view subverts the positive role the bow plays in the Genesis narrative and misinterprets the New Testament passages it leans on for support (e.g., 2 Pet 3:1-13).

Ecological concerns factor prominently throughout the Old Testament. Though they do not stand at the heart of Christian mission in the New Testament, they remain an important part of the witness of Israel and the Church to God's intentions for all creation. We will attend to such concerns briefly below and again as they factor into the storyline of Genesis.

The Flood and Theology

Most central to the missiological concerns of this volume are recent theological interpretations of the flood. By "theological" I mean what the flood account teaches us about God. In particular, scholars have wrestled with the flood account's seemingly violent depiction of God. Prior generations struggled most with the factual claims of the narrative: Did it really happen? This generation appears more concerned with the ethical implications of the narrative: How could a loving God do such a horrific thing? Though this question is certainly not new, it appears to be taking precedence over questions that previous generation found more pressing.

This new focus on divine violence may be connected to allegations against Christianity being raised by those whom Paul Copan calls the "new atheists."[108] These atheists have adapted their approach by seeking to prove that the Bible is at odds with itself and thus internally incoherent. Take, for example, the criticism of Richard Dawkins: "The legend of animals going into the ark two by two is charming, but the moral of the story of Noah is appalling. God took a dim view of humans, so he (with the exception of one family) drowned the lot of them including children and also, for good measure, the rest of the (presumably blameless) animals as well."[109] It is not lost on Dawkins that most Christians don't actually follow the moral example of God as depicted in this story; they prefer Jesus' teaching about love. So they pick and choose whatever suits them—just like they accuse atheists of doing.

Atheists are certainly not the only ones put off by the way God is depicted in Genesis 6-8. Many believers are, in fact, unsure how to deal with the flood's wide-sweeping carnage. Scholars have responded in a variety of ways. Some recycle well-worn responses of previous generations by claiming that the flood didn't really happen, so we don't really need to deal with it. Others concede that God is violent and fail to see a problem with that.

This generation approaches the text with a different set of sensibilities. They don't believe we can ignore the ethical implications of a biblical narrative just because it may not have happened historically. Whether history or mythology, they believe that all Scripture was meant to convey theological truth about God. Furthermore, many reject the notion that God is inherently violent and that we simply need to accept that fact, regardless of whether it rubs us the wrong way. They are convinced that the God of Genesis is none other than the God of Jesus. Since God has revealed himself most fully in Jesus, such that he is the exact representation of God (Heb 1:3), and since Jesus

---

[108] Paul Copan, *Is God a Moral Monster? Making Sense of the Old Testament God* (Grand Rapids: Baker, 2011), 15-23.

[109] Richard Dawkins, *The God Delusion* (Boston: Houghton Mifflin Company, 2006), 269.

reveals to us an "*agape*-centered, other oriented, self-sacrificial God who opposes violence and commands his people to refrain from violence,"[110] then portraits of divine violence in either Testament constitute an ethical and theological problem.

These sensibilities have resulted in a variety of different approaches to the question of divine violence and the flood.

1. God acted violently in flooding the earth. But he changed as a result and became less violent.[111]

2. God never acted violently in flooding the earth. Though the text presents him as having done so, we know that he didn't because Jesus reveals to us that he couldn't have acted violently.[112]

3. God flooded the earth. The text does not portray this as a divine act of violence, but as a necessary world-saving intervention.[113]

4. God did not flood the earth. The flood was about to happen as a natural disaster and God simply channeled it to accomplish his purposes.[114]

---

[110] Gregory A. Boyd, *Crucifixion of the Warrior God: Interpreting the Old Testament's Violent Portraits of God in Light of the Cross*, vol. 2, Cruciform Thesis (Minneapolis, MN: Fortress Press, 2017).

[111] Walter Brueggemann. *Genesis*, Interpretation: A Bible Commentary for Teaching and Preaching (Atlanta: John Knox Press, 1982), 73-87; Alan Dershowitz, *The Genesis of Justice: Ten Stories of Biblical Injustice that Led to the Ten Commandments and Modern Law* (New York: Warner Books, 2000), chs. 1 and 11.

[112] J. Denny Weaver, *The Nonviolent God* (Grand Rapids: Eerdmans, 2013), 90, 106-7, 124-32.

[113] Merilyn E. K. Clark. "A Flood of Justice: The Scope of Justice in the Flood Narrative (Gen. 6:5—9:19)," *International Journal of Public Theology* 3 (2009): 357-370; Jerome F. D. Creach, *Violence in Scripture*, Interpretation: Resources for the Use of Scripture in the Church (Louisville, KY: Westminster John Knox Press, 2013), 34-42.

5. God never acted violently in flooding the earth. God allowed authors to mischaracterize him as doing so, but all that God really did was stop holding back spiritual forces of chaos that threatened to destroy the earth so as to put an end to the systematic extermination of the human race by evil spirits who were procreating with humans.[115]

Such views have considerable merit. Though it is not clear that God became less violent after the flood, the text presents the flood as a one-time, non-repeatable event grounded in God's promise. Though it is not clear that God's self-revelation in Jesus means that he couldn't have possibly flooded the earth, scholars are right to view the flood account as disclosing the same God that we have come to know most fully in Jesus. Though the text overtly associates the flood with divine initiative, it is nonetheless true that it names natural forces as the active agents of destruction.

Though I am indebted to insights gleaned from these diverse perspectives, I take at face value that God took initiative in causing the flood, and I am not convinced that Genesis 6-8 portrays God as being capricious, murderous, or vengeful. On the contrary, the same divine love that sent

---

[114] Terence E. Fretheim, "The God of the Flood Story and Natural Disasters," *Calvin Theological Journal* 43 (2008): 21-34.

[115] Boyd, *Crucifixion of the Warrior God*, 1121-1142. Boyd's account is somewhat confusing insofar as he blames evil spiritual beings for the violence that filled the earth (in his interpretation of the sons of God) and he identifies evil spiritual forces as those that unleashed chaos upon the earth in the flood. God simply stopped protecting the earth from them. The end result is that evil spiritual beings wipe out the other evil spiritual beings that were beginning to take over the earth (1133-34). It seems as if the former would have had little vested interest in wiping out the latter. The analogy of God using wicked nations to wipe out other wicked nations doesn't resolve this issue. Babylon serves its own interests in defeating Assyria. What do the evil cosmic forces gain in wiping out the race of evil spiritual hybrids? Jesus faults the Pharisees for applying this sort of logic to his demon-exorcizing ministry (Matt 12:24-48).

Jesus to the cross also sent flood waters to the earth. This is not to ignore or minimize the tragedy of lost life recorded in this account, but to interpret it within its immediate and broader canonical context. I am not seeking to place the best possible spin on a troubling tale, but to understand the flood account on its own terms.

6:5-13 God Resolves to Flood the Earth and Spare Noah

God's Motive

The Genesis flood account begins with a double introduction: vv. 5-8 and vv. 9-13. These sections likely originated from two different sources, but that is not our concern. We are concerned with what they do and do not say in the combined form in which we now have them. It is common for scholars to attribute motives to God for flooding the earth that this passage does not convey. Denny Weaver, for example, interprets the flood as an act of divine vengeance, anger, and retaliation.[116] Yet this passage says nothing of the sort. It only says that God saw rampant wickedness and violence being perpetrated on the earth and that this brought him regret and grief. Only in this vein does God resolve to destroy nearly all living things. Nowhere does the flood account depict God as being angry. Language of fury, wrath, and revenge are strikingly absent.

It is true in human experience that anger often accompanies regret. Perhaps you've planned a party, invited guests, watched them trash your house or bicker with one another, regretted inviting them, and angrily asked them to leave. This sort of connection between regret and anger is all too common. But other scenarios exist. Suppose you adopt a pet, your children grow very close to it, a few months later it contracts rabies, you grieve that you have to put it to sleep, the whole family is devastated,

---

[116] Weaver, *Nonviolent God*, 90, 106-7.

and you regret ever bringing it home. In this scenario, anger doesn't accurately capture the mood or motive. It would be entirely inappropriate for someone to assume that you euthanized the dog as an act of vengeance. If self-centered humans are capable of genuine grief and regret, how much more the loving God revealed to us most fully in Jesus.

The Hebrew word used to describe God's grief (*atsav*) occurs three other times in Genesis. It describes the pain of a woman in childbirth (3:16), the pain of Jacob's sons when they heard that their father was partnering with the family responsible for raping their sister Dinah (34:7), and the painful remorse Joseph's brothers felt when they realized God was punishing them for selling their brother into slavery (45:5). All of these situations were deeply personal and entailed intense anguish. Alongside these accounts, we see even more clearly that God's disposition in flooding the earth was not bloodthirsty or vindictive as much as agonizing or excruciating.[117]

Human Violence

> **Urban Violence**
>
> The violence wrought from Cain onward which quickly wove its ways into his lineage is one of the hallmarks of cities that many point to today as reasons that (a) God disapproves of cities and (b) cities are the direct result of the fall. But is it that easy? Seemingly on a daily basis the local news details accounts of violence throughout the city. Stabbings, gun violence, domestic violence, vehicular homicide, and the like are some of the reasons why people point out things like "God is not in the city." As we see in these pre-flood accounts, when humanity drifts, it causes great grief to God. We can be assured, then, that cities (or

---

[117] In the case of Dinah's brothers, the intense grief was also accompanied by anger. But this anger was conveyed by a different word: *kharah*. Anger can accompany pain and lead to violent vengeance. But the term *atsav*, by itself, does not convey anger and retribution.

> any place where people live) are places where human violence grieves God. At the same time, we can be confident that God's *Imago Dei* is stamped upon every city dweller. The Holy Spirit is active. Before the rest of the city, God's people (i.e. the church) are actively living out what it means to be a covenant people in right relationship with God.
>
> *Sean Benesh*

When people tell the story of the flood, they often identify human wickedness as the root cause. That is certainly the case, but a specific form of wickedness is named: violence (vv. 11, 13). This should not be overlooked. In Genesis 1-11, violence is not simply one of many symptoms of creation's fallenness; it is arguably *the* central symptom. This is evident in the social consequences of sin, the social interactions following the fall, the events immediately preceding the flood, and the instructions God gives immediately after the flood.

Though other sins are mentioned, violence predominates. As a result of Adam and Eve's disobedience, enmity grows between the offspring of the serpent and the offspring of Eve. Serpents violently strike at human heels, and humans counter with deadly blows to their heads. Adam's relationship with the soil is equally antagonistic. The soil is stingy with its produce, humans must scratch at it with our sharpest instruments to harvest its fruit, and thorns and thistles find their own way to scratch back. Of course, the only consequence of sin that addresses how fallen humans relate to one another is that Eve's desire will be for her husband and that he will rule over her. This power struggle anticipates various persons with greater power using it to their own advantage at the expense of weaker parties. When the mere presence of the stronger party does not intimidate the weaker party into complying, violence is right around the corner.

This, you will recall, is exactly what happens in the three scenes of social interaction that follow the Fall and precede the flood. Cain murders Abel. Cain worries that wider society will try to kill him. God protects Cain with the threat of vengeance. Cain's near descendent, Lamech, takes multiple wives, kills a man, and uses God's approach to limiting violence to justify his own violence. This trend culminates in the sons of God who take many wives and surround themselves with mighty warriors who violently establish and maintain their rule.

In sum, Cain begat Lamech, Lamech begat multiple Lamechs, and multiple Lamechs dominated their subjects, warred against one another, and brought God's creation to its knees. This is why God floods the earth according to verse 13: "And God said to Noah, 'I have determined to make an end of all flesh, *for the earth is filled with violence because of them.*'" If that were not enough to demonstrate the centrality of violence to this account, immediately after the flood, God gives explicit instructions regarding the sacredness of blood and the lethal consequences of taking the lives of others (9:4-6).

The early chapters of Genesis therefore depict an epic struggle between God and a violent world. The flood is part of God's response to rampant violence. The strategic initiatives God implements after the flood seek further to curtail human violence. Ultimately, God's decision to form a people through Abraham's descendants to participate in his saving mission is part of God's strategic response to violence.

This does not mean violence remains the central sin all throughout the Bible story, though a strong case can be made that it's always near the top. At the very least, it cautions us against framing God's mission in ways that ignore the problem of violence altogether. In order to distance themselves from certain forms of pacifism, many believers short sell the peace dimension of Christian witness. Though the term "pacifism" has its problems (e.g., it sounds too passive and it has been coopted by theologically-anemic agendas), the theme of peace and violence is integral to the overarching Scriptural narrative and cannot be ignored.[118]

Creation's Fate

It is difficult to comprehend why God might destroy all of creation. But to truly enter into the world of this narrative is to enter a world in which wickedness reigns supreme, humanity is bent on evil all the time, violence goes unchecked, and "all flesh" appears to be in on it (vv. 12-13). The phrase "all flesh" may suggest that even animals and birds have entered into the violent ways of humans. This notion is supported by God's instruction after the flood, which holds humans *and* animals accountable for future bloodshed (9:5).[119]

The only innocent victim in this story, just like Genesis 3, appears to be inanimate creation. It has been corrupted by the violence perpetrated by all flesh, and now it will be destroyed along with all flesh (v. 13). Ecological readings are entirely appropriate at this point. Inasmuch as we are able to talk about the flood as the consequence of human violence upon the earth, we might also speak of Genesis 1-11 as the story of how human sin has negatively impacted inanimate creation.

We could talk about how humans were created to care for creation and commanded to respect the limits God placed on their dominion (Gen 1-2). Yet humans abused creation by transcending those limits, which led to a curse upon the soil (Gen 3). We could continue to explain how Cain's murder of Abel defiled the soil with innocent blood and how the first city was built upon the resulting estrangement from the soil and enabled more humans to

---

[118] John C. Nugent, "Beyond Pacifism and Militarism: A Canonical Approach to Christians and Warfare," *Stone-Campbell Journal* 19, no. 2 (Fall): 205-217.

[119] This does not mean that animals are morally accountable, which would contradict my interpretation of Gen 3. It may only mean that human violence incited animals to violence. The postdiluvian requirement to kill an animal that kills a human has no pedagogical value to the animal kingdom. It simply protects humans from an animal that is excessively dangerous, like a rabid dog.

remain in a perpetual state of estrangement (Gen 4). And now the whole earth has been corrupted by escalating human violence and must suffer the same fate as its culpable caretakers (Gen 6).

That the author did not want readers to interpret these chapters in a purely anthropocentric way is perhaps clearest after the flood when God resolves never again to curse the ground on account of human sin (8:21) and then covenants with *all living creatures* never to destroy the earth with a flood (9:11). Ecological readings are therefore a welcome and necessary emphasis in twenty-first century reflection on Genesis and mission.

6:14—7:5 Noah Builds and Enters the Ark

In the midst of judgment, we now catch a glimpse of God's grace. Creation has become utterly corrupt. All flesh has corrupted its ways upon the earth (6:12). Every thought of the human heart was always evil all the time (6:5). At this point, an all-powerful creator would have had several options:

- God could have wiped out the entire human race, all the animals, and perhaps even the planet. He could have re-started completely from scratch. But he didn't.

- God could have vanquished all living creatures and spared only the planet. He could have then created a new and improved variety of all species, exchanging sin-prone humans and blood-thirsty animals with flawless humans and toothless animals. But he didn't.

- God could have bypassed the flood altogether and stationed legions of powerful angels all throughout the earth. They could detect transgressors and swiftly punish them, thereby suppressing and deterring all future transgression. But he didn't.

Genesis gives no evidence that God entertained any of these options. Instead, he leaves his creation pretty much intact. By preserving Noah, his family, and at least two of each animal, God perpetuates all culpable species which had corrupted his good creation. What an affirmation of his original design!

God had already put his best foot forward, and nothing less would suffice. The human ability to do evil was no glitch. Something about it was worth preserving. Perhaps it is inseparably linked to our ability to do good and love freely. Be that as it may, God so the loved the world that he gave it another chance—all of it.

This supports the notion that God was not acting hastily or angrily when he flooded the earth. On the contrary, his desire to preserve every aspect of his original creation testifies that at least some elements of it were at risk. Had God not somehow intervened, they might have been lost forever.

God's Elect

Another dimension of this story ought not be overlooked, for it is central to a missional reading of Scripture. We have already noted that irresponsible humans stood at the center of creation's calamity. We also observed that God chose to stick with his original creation, warts and all. At this point we might expect God to set humans to the side, roll up his sleeves, and take care of business. God could easily create the ark himself, personally populate it with representatives of all creation, and then closely oversee their wellbeing during the lengthy flood.

But God is not like us. He didn't give up on his image. God declared his creation "very good" only after he created humans and gave them dominion in creation (Gen 1:31). In filling the earth with violence, wicked humans had not altogether disqualified themselves from this calling. So God selects one man and his family to head up his creation-preserving mandate. A man will build the ark (v. 14), take animals on the ark with him (v. 19), and gather enough food to keep all the creatures fed (v. 21). After initiating the flood waters, God appears to have taken a somewhat hands-off approach for multiple months (8:1). This left Noah and his family with a tremendous amount of responsibility. The future of the world population was on the line and God still calls upon fallen humans to carry the torch.

Of course, Noah was an exceptional man. His father prophesied of his future service to humanity (5:28-29). The Genesis author introduces him as "a righteous man, blameless in his generation"—a man who, like Enoch, "walked with God" (6:9). According to God, Noah is the last such man in existence (7:1). Should he die, there would be none righteous. Creation was down to its last godly man. So God confides in Noah and entrusts him with great responsibility.

Fortunately, God's confidence was not misplaced. Twice we are told that Noah did *all* that God commanded him (6:22; 7:5). The future of world history was riding on him. God had not tasked Noah with judging the world, flooding the world, or saving the world. God alone would do that. Noah's role involved assembling and preserving a faithful representative remnant. This pattern continues all throughout Scripture, and it is central to our understanding of Christian mission. Irresponsible humans pervert God's good gifts, and God calls to himself a remnant whose obedient response bears the future of world history.

The God who reveals himself to us in Scripture always has a partner in mission. God's election of Noah anticipates his later election of Abraham in Genesis 12. From that point forward, God's partner is tied to Abraham's lineage. Indeed, Abraham's progeny collectively is God's partner in mission for the rest of Scripture. Even when collectively they fail, God still identifies a faithful remnant of his people who will represent him to his people and, in turn, his people to the world. This pattern culminates in Jesus, the faithful son of Abraham, the exact representation of God to his people (Heb 1:3), the one who commissions and empowers God's people to represent God's will to all nations.

> **Spared Remnant**
>
> As we will continue to see throughout Scripture, this notion of a spared remnant is a powerful reminder of God's love for humanity and creation. God does not leave us alone! This motif of "called out ones" who live and act as faithful representatives is precisely what the church in the city is called to do today. We are to faithfully love and live in our neighborhoods and communities demonstrating before a watching world what it means and looks like to live in a covenant relationship with a loving God.
>
> Sean Benesh

7:6-24 Flood Waters Rise and Abate

As much comfort as we might take in creation's representatives floating providentially yet precariously upon the billows of the global swell—we are reminded toward the end of this passage of the gruesome carnage that befell all other living, breathing creatures.

It's no wonder Bible picture books focus on the impressive ark, the paired and spared animals, and the colorful rainbow. It would be overwhelming to focus on the deluge itself—on screaming children being rushed to higher ground; on the bloody battle royal that must have taken place at every high hill and elevated structure; and on every animal and human, young and old, quietly, eerily gasping for breath having lost the capacity for speech as water overtakes their lungs making it impossible for them to breath.

How could God's love shine through this grim, dismal reality? At this point in the narrative, it is easy to forget the divine grief with which the author introduced this account. We misread this account if we do. This story is not told as if God is sad at first and later gets mad, such that his anger gets the last word. Rather, God's grief is the narrative lens intended to help us view the entire account properly. Instead of reading the Bible backward from the vantage point of Calvary's cross asking how the loving God of Jesus could do such a thing, we should read this account forward by observing how deeply it must have grieved the creator to resort to such drastic measures to preserve his all-but-lost creation.

An analogy from the medical field may be instructive.[120] Imagine a doctor approaching a crestfallen husband about the tragic condition of his dying wife. They were late in detecting her cancer. It is rapidly metastasizing and will soon overtake her. She has, at most, one month to live.

Nothing can be done to save this woman, but she is seven months pregnant and the cancer has yet to compromise her baby's health. If they act fast, they may be able to extract the infant from her mother's womb. It is the child's only chance to survive, but the procedure is invasive enough that the now unresponsive mother is sure to die. The husband knows what must be done. His wife would gladly lay down her life so the baby might live. Grief-stricken, he assents to the procedure.

Of course, a description of what happens next is heart-wrenching. The doctor cuts open the woman's body. Blood flows profusely. Her pulse rapidly declines. She gasps for breath. The baby is spared, but her mother's body convulses its way toward a tragic death. As the husband kisses his wife's forehead for the last time, no one would question his motives for authorizing the death-dealing (but simultaneously life-saving) procedure. Likewise, no one would accuse the doctor of premediated murder.

If we can give fallible humans the benefit of the doubt in an extreme situation like this, how much more should we trust the loving creator of this world.

---

[120] I am grateful to my friend Steve Bush for suggesting this analogy during a weekly Bible study.

8:1-19 God Remembers All His Creatures

A new scene begins with divine remembrance. In noting that God remembered the ark's inhabitants, the Genesis author is not drawing attention to apparent divine amnesia. When the Pentateuch speaks about divine memory it means that God is once again tending to his people in a specific way, presumably to advance his purposes for them.

In Genesis 19:29, God remembers Abraham and chooses to spare Lot from the destruction of Sodom. In 30:22, God remembers Rachel and makes it possible for her to conceive and bear sons for Jacob. In Exodus 2:24, God remembers his covenant with the Patriarchs and begins acting to deliver the Israelites from Egyptian enslavement. In Leviticus 26:25, God vows to remember his covenant with his people and to spare them when they forsake his covenant.

For God to remember is for God to focus his attention. Divine attention usually means grace. Jonah knew this when God asked him to prophecy the destruction of Nineveh. He knew that any divine attention, even the threat of great loss, meant grace was near (Jonah 4:2). He didn't want God to extend such grace to Israel's enemies. So he attempted to flee God's presence in hopes that God would forget about the Ninevites and they would perish in their wickedness. That God remembers Noah and the animals therefore means that he intends to intervene on their behalf.

Aside from the theme of divine remembrance, Genesis 8:1-19 reveals little in the way of new theological or missiological information. It wasn't written to introduce brand new material as much as to recapitulate the material of two prior events. In doing so, it simultaneously closes out the flood event and opens up the story of new creation.

The Flood Redux

Genesis 8 recapitulates the first half of the flood account insofar as a deliberate literary pattern symmetrically juxtaposes the flooding and drying of the earth. This is evident in the events that propel the plot forward as well as the numbers that demarcate the time periods associated with the flood.

A - God *determines* to destroy the earth (6:11-13)
    B - Noah *builds* the ark (6:14-22)
        C - God tells Noah to *enter* the ark (7:1-5)
            D - Flood waters *rise* (7:6-24)
            D' - Flood waters *recede* (8:1-14)
        C' - God tells Noah to *exit* the ark (8:15-19)
    B' - Noah *builds* an altar (8:20)
A' - God *determines* to never again destroy the earth (8:21-9:17)

A - In *7 days* God will send rain (7:4)
    B - After *7 days* the flood comes (7:10)
        C - Flood continues *40 days* (7:17)
            D - Waters swell *150 days* (7:24)
            D' - Waters recede *150 days* (8:3)
        C' - Noah opens the window after *40 days* (8:6)
    B' - After *7 days* Noah sends out the dove (8:10)
A' - After *7 days* Noah sends out the dove (8:12)

This doubly chiastic structure testifies to the author's literary prowess and to God's deliberate activity in the flood. The year-long ordeal was not a matter of creation spinning out of control. Nor was it a random outburst of divine frustration. It was a carefully calculated divine response to human wickedness. To put it in concrete terms,

God was thoroughly purging the earth of serial molestation, rape, torture, slavery, theft, sex trafficking, assassinations, decapitations, and terrors of every imaginable kind.

Before the flood, God regretted creating humans (6:6). Afterward, he promised never to flood the earth again (8:21). Yet God never regrets sending the flood. It simply had to be done. It is tempting to say that the flood itself softened God's heart, as if he was mortified by what he had done and vowed never to commit such an atrocity again. But that's not how the Genesis author tells the story.

Before sending the flood, God told Noah he would make a covenant with him (6:18). The only covenant God makes with Noah is his postdiluvian covenant never to flood the earth again (9:8-17).[121] God knew—long before the flood— that this would be his one and only act of global destruction. He wasn't proud of what he had to do. As he says through the prophet Ezekiel, "I have no pleasure in the death of the wicked, but that the wicked turn from their ways and live" (Ezek 33:11). God took no pleasure in flooding the earth. It grieved him profusely precisely because he knew that it had to be done.

Creation Redux

The deliberate, almost tedious two-part structure of the flood narrative strongly echoes the numerically organized creation account of Genesis 1. Such reverberation is not incidental, according to Paul Kissling. He sees Genesis 8 as closely paralleling the first six days of creation.[122] The following chart organizes his evidence.

---

[121] Jeong Koo Jeon argues that God established two covenants with Noah: one before the flood and one after. His argument is unpersuasive. We engage it below in the context of Gen 9:1-7. See "The Noahic Covenants and the Kingdom of God," *Mid-America Journal of Theology* 24 (2013): 179-209.

[122] Kissling, *Genesis*, vol. 1, 303-11.

Precreation	God's wind or Spirit hovers over the waters (1:2)	God's wind or Spirit drives back the waters (8:1)
Day 1	God separates light from dark (1:3-5)	Cessation of rain restores normal cycles of light and dark (8:2)
Day 2	God separates waters above from waters below, creating the expanse of the sky (1:6-8)	Windows of heaven and fountains of the deep are closed, restoring the sky to its normal state (8:2)
Day 3	Waters gather, dry land appears, and vegetation grows (1:9-13)	Dry land begins to appear (8:5) and vegetation begins to grow (8:11)
Day 4	God sets luminaries in the sky (1:14-19)	Cessation of rain restores visibility to the luminaries (8:2)
Day 5	God populates the sky with birds and the seas with fish (1:20-23)	Noah releases birds into the sky (8:7-12)
Day 6	God populates the land with animals and humans (1:24-31)	Humans and animals return to land (8:17-19)
Procreation	Birds and land creatures commanded to be fruitful and multiply (1:22, 28)	Birds and land creatures commanded to be fruitful and multiply (8:17)

The point is simple and reinforces what we've said above: the flood is not the end of creation but its renewal. God didn't destroy this world; he destroyed what humans made of it. It is akin to a believer's rebirth in baptism (1 Pet 3:20-21). To pledge faith in Christ we must die to our old self. In the waters of baptism, we bury our sinful past and emerge new persons. Of course, the life we leave behind is precisely the life that is reborn. Our new identity is not a complete renunciation of our old self, but a solemn affirmation of the true self that God originally created us to be.

Likewise, God's very good creation was reborn in the flood. It reemerged with all the same potential for human thriving and human deprivation. God had not fundamentally changed what it means for humans to be humans, animals to be animals, and plants to be plants. God acknowledges this in 8:21, where he observes that the human heart remains evil from youth. This poses what are, perhaps, the most vital questions of the Genesis flood account: What will God ultimately do about the mess humans continually make of his good creation? What is his ultimate solution to human violence? What role will God's elect play in that solution? Answers to these questions get to the heart of God's mission in this world.

The flood account itself provides bits and pieces of such answers. Whatever God is going to do, he is not going to fundamentally change the interdependent, multifaceted nature of his very good creation. Whatever he is going to do, God is not going to strip humanity of their critical role as responsible caretakers and stewards of all creation. Whatever God is going to do, he will make special use of righteous people who walk with him while all others defy him.

Urban Rebuilding

Whatever we think of cities we know that after the flood humanity began urbanizing again. Cities were not simply some sinful aberration of life before the flood. City building picked up again post-flood. We can deduce from this one of two options: (1) cities still are accursed and the direct result of disobedient humanity or (2) cities were actually of divine intent as part of human flourishing and our call to steward creation. Often times the way we see these two options has a direct bearing on how we view cities and even our role within them.

Sean Benesh

Aftermath of Flood: 8:20—11:32

8:20-22 Noah's Altar and God's New Resolve

Noah's Offering

The first thing Noah does after disembarking is offer a series of sacrifices to God. This at least partly explains why God had asked him to take multiple pairs of clean animals onto the ark (7:2). Only clean animals were eligible for sacrifice. That God required him to make provisions for these future offerings suggests that they may have been God's idea and that Noah is once again doing as God commanded.

The purpose of the offerings is not explicit. Noah could simply be offering these animals as an act of thanksgiving. God kept faith with him and all other creatures whose lives he preserved on the ark. The flood was quite an ordeal, and Noah was certainly appreciative that God brought them all through it safely.

But that still doesn't explain the logic behind the offerings. What does killing and burning animals accomplish? In other Mesopotamian flood accounts, like the Epic of Gilgamesh, humans offered animal sacrifices to provide food for the needy gods. Yet Noah's God has no need for personal nourishment. It is more likely that Noah's sacrifices constituted a commitment to God.

When Israel offered sacrifices to God, they not only offered clean animals, but they also offered the best of their flocks: firstborn animals without blemish. The logic was simple. Humans are indebted to God for everything. He gives life, and he sustains all life with the sun, rain, and food, which we couldn't live without. We therefore owe God our best. We owe him righteous lives and faithful obedience. The best of their flocks and crops therefore represent human lives that are wholly devoted to God. They are the down payment for the righteous lives humans commit to live.[123]

Yet humans frequently renege on that commitment. God had to flood the earth precisely because humans utterly defiled it with their sinfulness.

So as soon as Noah disembarks, he makes a pledge to God. These exemplary animals represent the exemplary life that Noah and his family committed to living from then on. Whether as an act of gratitude, a recognition that all life belongs to God, or a pledge of righteous living, only the best would do because God is worthy of nothing less.

> **Offerings in Urban Centers**
>
> This theme of offering is key. Noah made a burnt offering before the Lord. We know that later on Israel offered the best (unblemished) animals and first fruits from their labor. This is part of giving our whole selves to God. These are the visible reminders that all we have is from the Lord. So what does it look like to give ourselves fully to God in the urban centers of today? What does a life that has been transformed by the gospel look like as we live out a life of gratitude and service to God?
>
> *Sean Benesh*

God's Response

God appreciates Noah's gesture. It rises to him as a fragrant aroma. But God is not naïve. He knows that humans will not live up to their best offerings. They are evil from infancy. Though the flood has cleansed the earth of sin, it has not destroyed the root of sinfulness: the human heart (8. 21).

As noted previously, this poses an acute problem. If humans haven't fundamentally changed, what will prevent a global relapse? Before the flood, God expressed his intention to shorten human lifespans, so that should help.

---

[123] For more on the logic behind Israel's sacrificial system, see John Howard Yoder, *Preface to Theology: Christology and Theological Method* (Grand Rapids: Brazos Press, 2002), ch. 12.

Purging the earth of wickedness also reset the clock and carved out time for implementing a longer term solution. Such a solution would not be necessary as long as God reserved the right to flood the earth every time things fall apart again. So God spares creation from enduring a fatalistic cycle of de-creation and recreation by resolving never to destroy the earth again.

God's world-sparing resolution can be interpreted in at least three different ways:

1. God could be committing to never destroy the earth as long as humans remain faithful to the covenant conditions God establishes for them.

2. God could be committing to never destroy the earth again by water.

3. God could be committing to never destroy the earth again, by any means.

The first two options are problematic. Option 1 depends on the covenant pericope including all of 9:1-17. Below I suggest several reasons why the covenant pericope should be limited to vv. 8-17. At this point, it will suffice to show the conceptual incoherence of this interpretation. In 9:8-17, God clearly covenants never to flood the earth again. In 9:1-7, he clearly commissions humans to be fruitful, multiply, and safeguard the blood of all creatures. If together they constitute a conditional, bilateral covenant, then God's promise to spare the world would depend on humans obeying his decrees.[124] Yet, in 8:21, God resolves not to curse the ground again "because of humankind" and then states how sinful humankind remains. Human violation of this so-called bilateral covenant therefore seems inevitable. It follows, then, that God will indeed

---

[124] This position is represented by Steven D. Mason, "Another Flood? Genesis 9 and Isaiah's Broken Eternal Covenant," *Journal for the Study of the Old Testament* 32, no. 2 (2007): 177-98.

curse the ground again because of humankind, contrary to v. 21.

Option 2 is slightly more plausible. Its plausibility is grounded in a few ambiguous qualifiers in the text. First, verse 21 indicates that God will never again curse the ground *because of humankind*. This leaves open the possibility that God may destroy the earth again, but for some other reason—perhaps due to the natural expiration of this world, his desire to create a brand new world, or his intention to whisk righteous humans away to a heavenly world. Second, verse 22 specifies that harvest cycles, seasons, and daily intervals will continue *as long as the earth endures*. This leaves open the possibility that once the earth stops enduring, these segmented time periods will also cease. The third qualifier appears in chapter 9. Verses 11 and 15 both indicate that God will never again destroy the earth *with a flood*. This leaves open the possibility that God will destroy the earth with something else, such as fire or perhaps a meteor.

The first problem with option 2 is anachronism. The threat of a meteor is a modern fear, not an ancient Israelite one. The threat of fire stems from a skewed reading of 2 Peter. It's a skewed reading because, whereas 2 Peter 3:7 anticipates judgment by fire, the stated outcome is the destruction of "the godless," not the planet and all living creatures. It is also skewed because Peter only mentions the "elements" being dissolved with fire and only the "heavens" as passing (3:10). By way of contrast, the fate of "the earth" is that everything done on it will be disclosed.[125] Second Peter never says that the earth will be destroyed by fire. Even if it did, the original audience of Genesis had no access to a New Testament prophecy that was first uttered long after their time and had no Old Testament precedent.

---

[125] Some translations (e.g., KJV) mislead by translating the word for "disclosed" as "burned up." For a helpful discussion on 2 Peter 3 and the wider theme of the earth's endurance, see Richard J. Middleton, *A New Heaven and a New Earth: Reclaiming Biblical Eschatology* (Grand Rapids: Baker Academic, 2014).

They would have been much more familiar with Old Testament prophets who anticipated the ultimate restoration of earthly things (Isa 11:6-10; 65:17-25; Mic 4:1-4; Ezek 47:8-12). It is also anachronistic to suggest that ancient Israelites believed the earth could be destroyed by something other than water. According to the cosmology of Genesis 1 and 7, creation entails separating and holding back the waters so habitable land may appear, and de-creation entails releasing the waters back to their original all-encompassing swell. Global conflagration and regeneration is a Stoic notion that Jews wouldn't encounter until much later, after Greek occupation.

The second problem with option 2 is that it doesn't cohere with the wider pericope. It would be quite anticlimactic for the account to read as follows: Noah offers a sacrifice, God is pleased with it, God recognizes that humans remain sinful and will likely mess things up again, and so he decides never again to use water to destroy all creatures. Avoiding water doesn't quite resolve the problem. The problem is that nonhuman creatures aren't ultimately to blame for widespread corruption; humans are, yet all creation suffered as a result.

Moreover, it would be a mere truism if, in the poem of verse 22, the author meant to say "as long as the earth endures, earthly things will endure." That's like saying, "As long as I am alive, I will be living." That's hardly a poem worth reciting. In reality, the original audience would have had no reason to think the earth would not endure forever. They weren't aware of global warming, and they didn't have nuclear weapons capable of obliterating the entire planet. More likely, the poem means that earthly cycles will continue uninterrupted as long as the earth still exists, which for them meant forever. This stands in contrast to the dramatic interruption represented by the flood. It is a hopeful thought that resolves the tension of innocent creatures suffering on account of the guilty.

Option three is therefore most likely: God was committing never to destroy the earth again, by any means. This is consistent with the canon of Scripture, which doesn't look for an absolute annihilation of the earth as the final point, but a restoration or renewal. Christian mission is therefore not about covering as many people as possible with "fire insurance." God's kingdom mission is much bigger than that, and it has a future place for the earth as well.[126]

> **Overcoming Fear**
>
> Today fears abound regarding some sort of global destruction or catastrophe. Because of the proliferation of media, including social media, we're more acutely aware of global happenings than ever before in human history. We know instantly of a bombing in London, an earthquake in Turkey, nuclear build-up in North Korea, and then the melting polar ice caps from global warming. Fear builds upon fear and media accentuates and reinforces these messages and makes them more widespread. Fear increases. Not only that, but seemingly every year Hollywood produces another blockbuster hit detailing the end of the world. However, we don't have to fear annihilation, but instead look forward to a restoration and renewal of our beloved planet.
>
> *Sean Benesh*

9:1-7 God's Blessing and New Restrictions

New Creation

Genesis 9:1-7 deliberately echoes Genesis 1:26-30. They both contain the commission to be fruitful, multiply, and fill the earth (1:28; 9:1, 7). Both assert that humans were made in God's image (1:26-27; 9:6). Both discuss the relationship between humans and nonhuman living

---

[126] I explore God's kingdom mission at length in *Endangered Gospel: How Fixing the World is Killing the Church* (Eugene, OR: Cascade Books, 2016). I also address the common misunderstanding that God has called Christians to rescue people from this earth and take us to a better place somewhere beyond this earth.

creatures (1:26, 28; 9:2). Both specify what humans may consume as food (1:29; 9:3).

These overt parallels send a clear message that God intended to make a new beginning after the flood. Yet God's new beginning is not a brand new or completely different creation. The new or renewed creation stands in fundamental continuity with the original creation. As destructive as the flood was, it washed away neither the sinfulness of the human heart (8:21), nor the fundamental goodness of God's creation.

Still, there are three noteworthy differences between Genesis 1 and 9. Whereas Genesis 1 presumes peaceful relations between humans and animals, God here places the fear and dread of humans upon all nonhuman creatures (9:2).[127] Whereas God provides plants to serve as food for humans and all living creatures in 1:29, he now stipulates that humans may eat animals (9:3). Whereas Genesis 1 says nothing about lifeblood, God gives specific instructions as to how humans may show proper respect for the blood of all living creatures (9:4-6).

Natural Law and the Covenant with Noah

In recent years, these differences have featured prominently in discussions about natural law and the so-called Noahic Covenant. Jeong Koo Jeon, for instance, argues that God made two covenants with Noah: a covenant of saving grace and a covenant of common grace.[128]

---

[127] The text does not say explicitly that *God* placed the dread of humans on animals, but it is a reasonable conclusion. The text introduces animal dread of humans as a new thing. The fact that God forbids the consumption of animal blood immediately after the flood suggests that humans were consuming it before the flood. If human aggression alone were the initial cause of animal dread, it would thus have been present before the flood and not a new thing here. This leaves God as the most likely agent.

[128] Jeong Koo Jeon, "The Noahic *Covenants* and the Kingdom of God," *Mid-America Journal of Theology* 24 (2013): 179-209.

God shows saving grace to Noah and his family by sparing their lives on the ark. This antediluvian covenant parallels God's later covenants with Abraham, Moses, and Israel. Like them, it is particularistic insofar as it focuses on one man and his family (6:18), and it entails a distinction between clean and unclean foods (7:2).[129] Because this covenant is redemptive, it parallels the saving grace God has extended through Christ. This is why the Apostle Peter links the salvation of Noah with salvation in Christ (1 Pet 3:18-22).

By way of contrast, God's postdiluvian covenant extends common grace. This much is clear, Jeon argues, in that God makes this covenant with *all* people and creatures (9:12) and God makes no distinction between clean and unclean animals as food (9:3). Jeon also refers to this covenant as a covenant of preservation. God preserves order and life throughout the world by legislating that whoever kills someone must be killed. Jeon believes the covenant is universal and therefore binding until the end of time. For this reason postdiluvian edicts, like capital punishment, remain enforceable until the return of Christ.[130]

David VanDrunen also views the postdiluvian covenant as a covenant of preservation, though he doesn't make much of the antediluvian covenant.[131] For him, the strong links

---

[129] This argument is extremely speculative. The only function clean animals appear to fulfill in the Noah account is that they are sacrificed as whole burnt offerings after the flood. Such offerings are not eaten. Furthermore, in 6:21 the food that Noah stores on the ark is different from the animals he takes on the ark. The point of God allowing humans to eat all animals in 9:3-4 is not that humanity is leaving behind a distinction between clean and unclean food laws, but that they are moving beyond the plant only diet established in 1:29-30. Indeed, it is not even clear that God made a covenant with Noah before the flood. It is true that he plans to spare Noah and the animals on the ark, but not every plan God makes with people is a covenant. It is most likely that language of covenant in 6:18 anticipates the covenant that God makes only after the flood.

[130] Jeon, "The Noahic *Covenants*," 205-9.

between Genesis 1 and 9, as well as the universal and permanent scope of God's covenant with Noah, mean that the edicts of this chapter constitute natural law. They are eternally binding and grounded in God's created order. They thus furnish an ethic for governing authorities who are tasked with the role of protection. At the heart of this ethic is the concept of proportionality. Language of "blood for blood" (9:6) is not so much about capital punishment, for Van Drunen, as it is about administering punishments that fit the crime—no more and no less.[132] The state is not tasked with redeeming or creating an ideal society; it is tasked with protecting society from those who threaten its stability and peace. He thus sees a clean division of responsibility between God's people, who participate in God's redemptive mission according to redemptive ethics (e.g., turn the other cheek), and the state, which oversees God's protective mandate according to proportional ethics.[133]

Though some of their observations have merit, Jeon and VanDrunen's covenantal approaches to Genesis 9:1-7 are misguided.[134] One reason is that this passage is not actually part of the Noahic covenant pericope. All scholars agree that 9:8-17 is part of God's covenant with Noah. It begins by forthrightly stating, "As for me, I am establishing my covenant with you" (v. 9) and ends by saying, "This is the sign of the covenant that I have established" (v. 17). In

---

[131] David VanDrunen, "Natural Law in Noahic Accent: A Covenantal Conception of Natural Law Drawn from Genesis 9," *Journal of the Society of Christian Ethics* 30, no. 2 (2010): 131-49; and "The Protectionist Purpose of Law: A Moral Case from the Biblical Covenant with Noah," *Journal of the Society of Christian Ethics* 35, no. 2 (2015): 101-117.

[132] VanDrunen, "Protectionist Purpose," 105.

[133] VanDrunen, "Protectionist Purpose," 110.

[134] My understanding of this passage has been enriched by Josh Bush's fine paper delivered at the 2017 Stone-Campbell Journal Conference in the student paper competition, "Elastic Covenant: The Dangers of Elongating the Noahic Covenant."

between, we have an unambiguous statement as to the content of this covenant: "I establish my covenant with you, that never again shall all flesh be cut off by the waters of a flood to destroy the earth" (v. 11). Then, in verses 12-17, God specifies that the rainbow serves as a sign of this covenant never to destroy the earth again by water.

By way of contrast, language of covenant appears nowhere in 8:20—9:7. Rather, in 8:20-22, we hear of God's internal resolve never to destroy the earth again and, in 9:1-7, we have divine stipulations for populating the earth in ways that respect the sacredness of life. If the author intended these earlier sections to be part of his covenant stipulations, he did little to concretely connect them. In fact, the phrase "be fruitful and multiply," which occurs at the beginning and end of 9:1-7, serves as an *inclusio*—a literary device designed to set this section apart from what precedes and succeeds it.

Steven Mason believes he has found deliberate covenant linkage between 1-7 and 8-17.[135] He correctly notes that the covenant in Genesis 17 uses the phrase "as for me" to introduce God's responsibility in the covenant and the phrase "as for you" to introduce Abraham's responsibility in the covenant. He then observes that 9:1-7 ends by saying "and you" and 9:8-17 contains the phrase "as for me" (v. 9), thereby linking the two sections. He thus interprets 9:1-17 as a bilateral covenant that stipulates terms for both parties. This verbal correspondence is intriguing, but not convincing. Unlike 17:9, the phrase "and you" appears at the end of the section (v. 7 of 9:1-7) and is in no way associated with covenant language. Furthermore, when we read v. 7 in the context of 1-7 we see that it applies *only* to the command to be fruitful and multiply and that it addresses *only* Noah and his sons. By way of contrast, the phrase "as for me" in v. 9 is unambiguously tied to the

---

[135] Steven D. Mason, "Another Flood? Genesis 9 and Isaiah's Broken Eternal Covenant," *Journal for the Study of the Old Testament* 32, no. 2 (2007): 177-98.

covenant God is making, and v. 10 makes it clear that God is making this covenant not only with Noah and his sons, but also with every living creature (v. 10). That all living creatures are party to this covenant is reiterated in vv. 12, 15, 16, and 17.

VanDrunen's linkage isn't much stronger. He affirms Mason's problematic argument and adds to it only that 8:20-22 is similar to 9:8-17 in substance, insofar as both passages discuss God's resolve never to destroy the earth.[136] VanDrunen then assumes that all of 8:20—9:17, including 9:1-7, is covenantal. Yet this simply does not follow. The end of chapter 8 records God's inward resolution. Though this leads him to make a covenant later when he addresses Noah and his sons, this does not therefore make it part of the covenant. It is simply part of the narrative that lays the groundwork for the later covenant. By VanDrunen's logic, the Exodus 14 narrative about the crossing of the Red Sea should be considered part of Moses' song about the Red Sea crossing in Exodus 15. After all, both chapters are similar in substance.

Capital Punishment

At this point, you may be wondering why it even matters whether 9:1-7 is part of the Noahic covenant. There are several reasons, but we will focus on two, beginning with the biblical basis for capital punishment. The covenant established in 9:8-17 is a universal, everlasting covenant for all future generations (vv. 12, 16). To include vv. 1-7 is therefore to make its stipulations to procreate, eat animals, and kill killers eternally binding. This is exactly what we see Jeon do with the practice of capital punishment.[137]

---

[136] VanDrunen, "Natural Law in Noahic Accent," 133. See also fns. 9-10 on p. 147. VanDrunen agrees with Mason that the phrases "as for you" and "as for me" link the two sections together as a single covenant, but he disagrees that this makes the covenant conditional. God will keep his end, VanDrunen affirms, regardless of whether humans keep theirs (134).

Theologians have long used such logic to undermine Christian arguments against the death penalty.[138]

Yet a strong case can be made that the shedding of blood stipulated in v. 6 is a cultic or ceremonial act. The instructions about draining an animal's blood lay a foundation for Israel's sacrificial system. Early on in Israelite history, every animal that was slain—even for a common meal—had to be brought before a priest (Lev 17:1-5). Torah also teaches that human bloodshed defiles the land and the death of the killer is required in order to make atonement: "You shall not pollute the land in which you live; for blood pollutes the land, and no expiation can be made for the land, for the blood that is shed in it, except by the blood of the one who shed it" (Num 35:3). In this light, the shedding of a killer's blood in Genesis 9:6 serves to atone for the act of bloodshed.

That being the case, the work of Christ may be relevant to Christian convictions about the practice of capital punishment. John Howard Yoder represents this position well:

> It is the clear testimony of the New Testament, especially of the Epistle to the Hebrews, that the ceremonial requirements of the Old Covenant find their end—both in the sense of fulfillment and in the sense of termination—in the high-priestly sacrifice of Christ. "Once for all" is the good news. Not only is the sacrifice of bulls and goats, turtledoves and wheatcakes at an end; the fact that Christ died for our sins, once for all, the righteous one for the godless (Heb. 9:26–28; 1 Pet. 3:18), puts an end to the entire expiatory system, whether it be enforced by priests in Jerusalem or by execution[ers] anywhere else.[139]

---

[137] Jeon, "The Noahic *Covenants*," 205-209. He is not alone.

[138] This is the position of Wayne House in his debate with John Howard Yoder, *The Death Penalty Debate* (Dallas: Word Publishing, 1991), 103.

Yoder's point is simple and may be presented syllogistically:

- If the biblical basis for capital punishment is Genesis 9:6—and most death penalty advocates place it here rather than in Torah, since Torah is specific to Israel and includes things like dishonoring parents and the sabbath day,
- and if Genesis 9 is speaking about a cultic sacrificial practice,
- and if Jesus put an end to all cultic sacrificial systems,
- then Jesus also put an end to the practice of atoning for human bloodshed.

This is why it is so important for death penalty advocates to view 9:6 as being part of an everlasting covenant.

Here is not the place to settle the death penalty debate, but we can at least appreciate how a simple exegetical decision, like whether or not 9:1-7 is part of the covenant named in 9:8-17, might impact situations in which people's lives are on the line. There was a time when wider American society was moving away from the practice of capital punishment. Sadly, Christians were a significant factor in stemming that tide—precisely because of a misreading of this passage.

Dual Ethic

A second reason why lumping 9:1-7 in with the eternal covenant of 9:8-17 matters is that scholars like VanDrunen use it as the basis for constructing a natural law ethic that competes against the ethic of Christ. VanDrunen laments that Protestants have historically avoided natural law reasoning. He sees his interpretation of Genesis 8-9 as laying a biblical foundation for a natural law ethic that should appeal to them.[140] Yet Christian ethicists know what

---

[139] John Howard Yoder, *End of Sacrifice*, 102-103.

is at stake, and at least part of what is at stake is the shape of Christian witness.

Natural law theorists have long argued for a dual ethic that is rooted in a two kingdoms framework.[141] According to this position, the governing authorities rule over the kingdoms of this world according to the dictates of natural law, and Christ rules over the kingdom of God according to the principles that he lived and taught. Natural law advocates propose that Christians should abide by the way of Christ in their church, home, and private life, and that those same Christians should abide by the dictates of natural law while serving the common good in the public realm. Within such a framework, Christian witness entails setting aside the way of Christ within those realms where believers most frequently interact with unbelievers.

There is another way to view natural law according to theologians like Stanley Hauerwas.[142] Standing on the shoulders of Karl Barth and John Howard Yoder, Hauerwas argues that we should not sharply distinguish between the way of Christ and the way of nature. Citing Scriptures like John 1:3, Colossians 1:16-17, and Hebrews 1:2, he argues that the natural world came into existence through Christ and that his ways are identical to the ways

---

[140] VanDrunen, "Natural Law in Noahic Accent," 131-32.

[141] See Martin Luther, *Secular Authority: To What Extent It Should Be Obeyed*, in *Martin Luther: Selections from his Writings*, ed. John Dillenberger (New York: Doubleday, 1962), 363-402. Though Luther was instrumental in the Protestant Reformation, he grew up Roman Catholic and his ethical framework was heavily influenced by it. Calvin moved further away from this framework with his rejection of natural law, but he still maintained a two kingdoms framework that amounted to much the same thing.

[142] Stanley Hauerwas, *With the Grain of the Universe: The Church's Witness and Natural Theology* (Grand Rapids: Baker, 2001). For a summary of Hauerwas' approach to natural law, see my paper delivered at the 2011 Christian Scholars Conference in Malibu, CA, http://www.walkandword.com/writings/index.php?cat=1&id=11.

that creation was always meant to be. Since God created all things through Christ, to live the way of Christ is to live with the grain of the universe. His way is the way things were created to be, the way they will be when God renews creation at the Parousia, and the way the Church must live if we are to bear witness to God's kingdom and draw all people to it. Furthermore, the way of Christ is relevant in all things because God has made him first in all things, all things are being subjected to him, and all things hold together in him.[143] This constitutes a much different foundation for Christian mission in the public realm.

If Hauerwas is right about Christ, then natural law advocates routinely identify behaviors that are not actually natural—but rather the negative consequences of sin—and accord them natural status. That is precisely what VanDrunen does with Genesis 9:1-7. In these verses, God strives to curtail the violence of antediluvian society. He does so by causing animals to fear humans so they will have a fighting chance of escaping capture. God concedes that, in a world where animals die, humans will eat them. So he permits it with an important qualifier: humans must at least regard animal life as sacred by draining their blood, which contains their life (Lev 17:11).

God also concedes that killing is going to continue in a fallen world and that people will respond to it by multiplying vengeance (e.g., Lamech's seventy sevenfold vendetta in Gen 4:24). So he restricts violence to life for life, blood for blood. Only the killer gets killed. There is nothing natural about this. Rather, it represents necessary partial movement away from unnatural indiscriminate killing back toward the truly natural state of no killing at all. Jesus fulfills this movement by walking unnatural

---

[143] Branson Parler does an excellent job making this point in his engagement of John Howard Yoder in *Things Hold Together: John Howard Yoder's Trinitarian Theology of Culture* (Harrisonburg, VA: Herald Press, 2012).

retaliation all the way back to a state of nonretaliatory peace:

> ³⁸ You have heard that it was said, 'An eye for an eye and a tooth for a tooth.' ³⁹ But I say to you, Do not resist an evildoer. But if anyone strikes you on the right cheek, turn the other also; ⁴⁰ and if anyone wants to sue you and take your coat, give your cloak as well; ⁴¹ and if anyone forces you to go one mile, go also the second mile. ⁴² Give to everyone who begs from you, and do not refuse anyone who wants to borrow from you. ⁴³ "You have heard that it was said, 'You shall love your neighbor and hate your enemy.' ⁴⁴ But I say to you, Love your enemies and pray for those who persecute you, ⁴⁵ so that you may be children of your Father in heaven; for he makes his sun rise on the evil and on the good, and sends rain on the righteous and on the unrighteous. (Matt. 5:38-45)

Jesus isn't the only one who anticipated that, in the kingdom, these unnatural practices would be reversed. Even though God instilled the dread of humans into animals and permitted humans to eat their meat, that didn't mean this was natural or the way things were meant to be. Genesis 9:2-3 identifies it as a shift away from God's original harmony and plant-based diet.[144] Animals, of course, aren't the only ones who fear. Genesis 9:5 proclaims a reckoning for animals who kill humans precisely because animals, too, are predators that kill and consume the lifeblood of humans. Yet the prophets recognized that this isn't the way it's supposed to be. They

---

[144] For vegetarian interpretation of this passage and a helpful survey of alternative explanations for why God permitted the eating of animals, see Yael Shemesh, "Vegetarian Ideology in Talmuidic Literature and Traditional Biblical Exegesis," in *Genesis*, Texts @ Contexts Series (Minneapolis: Fortress, 2010), 107-127.

[145] Cf. Richard Whitekettle, "Freedom from Fear and Bloodshed: Hosea 2.20 (Eng. 18) and the End of Human/Animal Conflict," *Journal for the Study of the Old Testament* 37, no. 2 (2012): 219-236.

foresee a future day when God restores the original peace and harmony between animals and humans (e.g., Isa 11:6-9; 65:25; Hos 2:18).[145]

It is therefore a questionable practice to pit "natural" law against the way of Jesus. It is even more questionable to ask Christians to set aside the way of Jesus in certain areas of life and to adopt another standard that is allegedly rooted in nature but is actually rooted in practical guidance for how to mitigate the harmful effects of sin in a fallen world. This is analogous to how Jesus deals with the issue of divorce. Though Scripture regulates the practice by placing restrictions on it (Deut 24:1-4), we ought not think of it as natural. When the Pharisees bring Jesus into that conversation, he informs them that the Old Testament regulations were a necessary stop-gap measure and that from the beginning it was not God's intentions (Matt 19:8).

But natural law theorists like VanDrunen and Luther are attuned to something important. They want to know what kind of behavior we should expect of people who work for the kingdoms of this world and are not committed to the way of Jesus. Their sincere attempt at searching the Scriptures for such insight is admirable. Unfortunately, the Scriptures don't provide instructions for how to be a "good" unbeliever or how to manage the kingdoms and structures of this world that are passing away. It is admirable to seek common ground with fallen structures and their managers, but it is misguided to think that Scripture prescribes a common law code that we can confidently decipher, whether the Ten Commandments (as Luther held) or Old Testament civil code (as Calvin held).

Christian mission will indeed send us into situations where we must find common ground and cooperate with unbelievers as we seek the common good. But if they are to truly occupy common ground with us, for whom Christ is first in all things, then such ground will overlap with the way of Christ. So we must always invite unbelievers into the way of Christ. We dare not lead them anywhere else. The middle ground between believers and unbelievers is not an abstract moral code superimposed upon the

Scriptures, but the space between wherever unbelievers happen to be and the place where believers already are in Christ. We should only invite them to take the next possible step toward Christ and his kingdom, whatever that step might be. We won't expect them to do this, since they remain in rebellion. We won't command them to do this, since God's offer in Christ is a gift that they are free to accept or reject. But we won't do anything less, since anything less is not the calling we have received in Christ.

> **Common Good of the City**
>
> Towards the end of this section there is helpful insight that pertains to the practical world of seeking the common good of the city. Since this is not reserved solely for the church it means that we rub shoulders and link arms with people who do not profess Christ nor follow his way. We are freed up to come alongside, love alongside, and serve alongside all the while we lovingly invite them to take a step towards Christ and his kingdom.
>
> Sean Benesh

Concession to Human Sinfulness

If Genesis 9:1-7 is not part of the Noahic Covenant, the beginnings of a natural law code, or a blueprint for statecraft, then what exactly is it? What function does it fulfill in the ongoing narrative of Genesis 1-11? I've alluded to it above in piecemeal fashion, but it bears repeating here in a clear way that is disentangled from contemporary debates.

Before chapter 9, we saw human sin plunge this world into a state of perpetual corruption and violence. This grieved God, who began a series of strategic initiatives that would set this world on a better course without stripping it (or humanity) of what was very good about it in the first place. His first initiative was to limit lifespans to 120 years. That would at least cap the amount of evil one powerful person could do. Next, he wiped all wickedness off the face of the earth while preserving representatives of all living creatures. He thus kept the original creation intact while creating time to implement his other strategic initiatives.

Because humans remained sinful even after the flood and because God resolved not to simply wipe everything out again every time things got bad, God sought to limit further the amount of violence their sinfulness would generate. According to 9:2, therefore, he gave animals a fighting chance to escape human violence by placing the fear and dread of humans upon them. In 9:3-4, he granted humans permission to eat dead animals, but heightened their sensitivity to the sacredness of animal life by requiring them to drain animal blood before consuming them. Since animal blood and life is sanctified in this way, how much more that of humans! God then placed additional restraints upon human bloodshed by limiting retaliation to one life for one life. In light of these new restrictions, God reaffirms his world-populating mandate to be fruitful and multiple upon the earth.

Upon receiving these restrictions, God's people did not translate them into all languages and disperse them to all governing authorities so they might know how to carry out their God-given responsibility. It would never have dawned upon the original author or audience that God's people might be in a position to tell powerful world empires how to operate. Even those few Israelites in the Old Testament who had an audience with pagan rulers—like Joseph, Moses, Daniel, Nehemiah, and Esther—made no effort to share these restrictions with them. Rather, God's people viewed them as informing their own calling as God's set apart people. Respect for animal blood informed their farming, hunting, eating, and sacrificial practices. Respect for human life informed their own laws and relationships with their neighbors. Like everything else in Genesis 1-11, they viewed these chapters as foundational for understanding why their world was so broken, why God set them apart as his chosen people, and how they might order their lives according to their mission to be God's blessing to all nations.

These restrictions are not the last of God's strategic initiatives. One of the most significant initiatives comes in chapter 11. Those who wish to find how God uses the nations as a part of his work of preserving a tolerable level of stability and peace in this world are better off looking there. So we will return to this discussion in our commentary on chapter 11.

9:8-17 God's Covenant with All Creation

Much of what needs to be said about 9:8-17 has already been said in previous sections. These verses stand as a unified section with a clearly delineated beginning and ending and a consistent theme throughout. What God internally resolved to do in 8:21-22, he now externally pronounces to Noah and his sons. In that passage, he had resolved never again to curse the ground on account of humans. Now he establishes a covenant never again to spoil the earth and all living creatures.

God's Creation

> **Symbols of Grace in the City**
>
> In the same way rain is a precious gift of God and a symbol of his grace we can make the case that all around us are the "symbols of grace" in the city. That can range from free public schools, free lunches for lower income students, free healthcare for those in economic need, public transit, sewers, clean water as a basic human right, and many other things we take for granted. We can identify and note cities and countries where these kinds of services and essentials are available as well as other places where they are not. There are many blessings right under our noses.
>
> *Sean Benesh*

What stands out most in this passage are repeated statements that this covenant is not only with humans (vv. 9, 11, 12, 15), but with all living creatures (vv. 10, 12, 15, 16, 17) and earth itself (v. 13). The sheer repetition appears to be intentional. It underscores that nonhuman creatures are genuine participants in this covenant. The reason for this may be evident in God's internal resolve in 8:21-22. The earth did not deserve the destruction it had to endure. The divine image bearers who were tasked with serving and guarding the earth were responsible for bringing the earth to the brink of desolation.

The language of this covenant therefore packs a punch of shame. In essence, God is saying to Noah and his sons, "It's not all about you!" God cares deeply for all creation and, from this point forward, he intends to look after all creation, in order to protect it—from humans! It is interesting that the bow in the clouds is something that *God* will see (v. 16) and that it causes *God* to remember his covenant. This should throw anthropocentric (human-centered) readers a bit off balance. If this covenant were all about us, then we might expect the sign in clouds to remind *us* that God will not do something to harm *us* ever again. So when we are told that *God* is watching over his creation and that *he* won't forget his covenant with all creation, we should expect that when humans begin to cross the line again, God will go directly to the root of the problem. Nonhuman creation will no longer suffer as the collateral damage of divine judgment. This covenant should therefore occupy a prominent place in ecological interpretations of Scripture. It is one of the strongest affirmations of creation's value, independent of its usefulness to humans.

That said, we should not miss the grace of God conveyed by this covenant. Rain was a precious gift from God. It replenishes the earth's water supply and sustains all crops and flocks. In the Fertile Crescent, rainy seasons were typically quite long, spanning a good deal of the winter season and then drying up for an even longer spell. Each year, the rain would have shut God's people in for quite some time. This is something they celebrated because it replenished their water supply for the year. Yet, with the flood, rain became synonymous with wide-sweeping death. Without a covenant that God would never flood the earth again, humans may have lived in fear every time rainfall lingered a bit longer than usual. We might legitimately wonder, "Was God doing it again? Have we gone too far in our wickedness?" Apart from God's promise, this source of abundant blessing could have become another source of superstition and terror.

God's Sign

The other prominent feature of this passage, which we have yet to discuss, is the precise nature of the "bow" that God hung in the clouds.[146] The word for bow in this passage (*qesheth*) most often means the primary death-dealing implement in warfare and hunting (e.g., Gen 27:3; 48:22). For God to hang his bow in the sky may therefore signify that, having waged war against creation on account of human sinfulness, God now retires his weapon of mass destruction. This meaning is simple and perfectly complements the unfolding narrative with its emphasis on the problem of violence, God's grief that he has to suppress violence with violence, and his command that humans limit their own violent retaliation. God now leads by example by hanging up his bow and waging peace against a violent world.

Yet surely this term means more than a primeval weapon. This bow appears with the clouds both spatially (v. 13-14, 16) and temporally (v. 14, 16). Given that the rainbow goes by the same term (cf. Ezek 1:28), that it stretches across the sky, and that it most often appears after rainfall, it is difficult to imagine that the author did not intend readers to associate it with the resplendent, multicolored arch.

The Genesis author most likely meant both. When the rainbow appears in the sky, both God and humans will recall how God retired his globally-destructive arsenal. Yet surely an arched rainbow can call to mind a weapon that God once wielded and will never wield again.

---

[146] For a helpful summary of the range of meanings, see Paul J. Kissling, "The Rainbow in Genesis 9:12-17: A Triple Entendre?" *Stone-Campbell Journal* 4 (2001): 249-261.

The meaning of this term need not be limited to these two senses according to Paul Kissling. The arch of the rainbow may also have reminded ancient readers of the arch-shaped firmament.[147] Several Old Testament passages suggest that ancient Israelites viewed the sky, much like their contemporaries, as a semi-circular dome (Ezek 1:22-28; Job 22:14; 26:10; Isa 40:22; Prov 8:27). In creation, that dome was made to separate the waters above from the waters below. In the flood, God allowed that dome to collapse so the earth was deluged from above and from below. After the flood, the waters returned to their places and the dome was restored. So it is quite possible that whenever God sees his arch-shaped bow in the clouds, he will remember to keep his arch-shaped dome intact to protect his very good creation. Kissling's main point is not that the firmament interpretation is the single right interpretation, but that the author may have chosen the rich term *qesheth* to serve as a triple entendre that brings all three senses to mind.

9:18-28 Noah's Cursed and Blessed Sons

On the surface, it appears that the flood account is finally behind us. The narrative picks up with postdiluvian life. But upon closer examination, this pericope actually wraps up the wider story of de-creation and re-creation that revolves around the flood. As 9:1-7 parallels chapter 1, so 9:18-28 parallels chapters 2-3. Divine promises and commissions are followed by human response. What do people do when God withdraws his creative presence and they are seemingly on their own?

The parallels are quite remarkable. Noah was a man of the soil who worked a vineyard; Adam's name literally means soil and he worked the garden in Eden. Noah drank of the fruit of the vine and became naked; Adam and Eve ate of from the fruit of a tree and realized they were naked. Ham meddled, took advantage of Noah's vulnerability, and his

---

[147] Kissling, "Rainbow in Genesis 9:12-17," 259-260.

offspring were cursed; the serpent meddled, took advantage of Adam and Eve's vulnerability, and his offspring were cursed. Shem is elevated over Ham, and Noah's account comes to an end; Adam is elevated over Eve, and Adam's account comes to an end.

These parallels are too strong to ignore, and the message is not difficult to decipher. God was right; when it comes to the human heart, the flood didn't change a thing. It is evil from youth (8:21). Immediately after God withdraws, the new first family falls into a state of dysfunction. It all began, once again, with poor stewardship of nonhuman creation. Ecological concerns remain integral to the author's agenda.

Ham's Offense

More difficult to decipher is the precise nature of Ham's offense. Genesis 9:22 is notoriously vague about what Ham did to Noah. We are only told that he saw his father's nakedness and told his two brothers. His brothers then covered their father and, after he woke up, Noah cursed Ham's son Canaan. These clues are cryptic enough that readers may be expected to read between the lines. This has led to five different theories:[148]

1. Castration. The least popular theory is that Ham castrated his father. This position requires the most reading between the lines. When he wakes up, Noah realizes what his son had "done" to him. What Ham did follows from the fact that he saw his father naked. Because Ham denied Noah the privilege of having additional children, Noah curses him by making life miserable for Ham's own child: Canaan. In support of this theory, Noah does not appear to have had

---

[148] For helpful surveys and evaluations of these views, see John Sietze Bergsma and Scott Walker Hahn, "Noah's Nakedness and the Curse on Canaan (Genesis 9:20-27)," *Journal of Biblical Literature* 124, no. 1 (25-40); and Nicholas Odhiambo, "The Nature of Ham's Sin," *Bibliotheca Sacra* 170 (Apr-Jun 2013): 154-65.

additional children according to the genealogy of chapter 10, despite the fact that God twice commissioned him to be fruitful and multiply (9:1, 7). Nothing else in Genesis and the wider Pentateuch supports this interpretation.

2. Voyeurism. A more popular theory requires perhaps the least amount of reading between the lines. It takes the words of the text at face value. Ham looked inappropriately upon his father's nakedness and invited his brothers to do the same. It is inappropriate to lust over one's father in this way, so when Noah finds out he curses Ham's son. Though cursing his grandson seems disproportionate to the offense, it has less to do with the man Canaan and more to do with his distant descendants, the Canaanites, who looked inappropriately upon one another, which led to all sorts of sexual improprieties.[149]

3. Negligence. This theory offers a minor tweak of the voyeurism theory. The text does not say that Ham lusted after his father. His offense was his failure to cover his naked father. What is worse, he told others about Noah's nakedness. That he should have kept his mouth shut and covered his father is evident in the response of Ham's brothers who took great care to cover their father without looking upon his nakedness (v. 23). His brothers' actions implicitly critique Ham's negligence. Though Noah's punishment of Ham's son seems excessive, Odhiambo argues that the wider canonical context considers Ham's behavior a big deal.[150]

---

[149] Brad Embry, who advocates the voyeurism view, also deems the curse appropriate because of the way it replays Genesis 3. Since Adam and Eve discovered their nakedness, are covered, and are subsequently cursed, it follows that Noah after being seen naked, would issue a curse after being covered. "The 'Naked Narrative' from Noah to Leviticus: Reassessing Voyeurism in the Account of Noah's Nakedness in Genesis 9.22-24," *Journal for the Study of the Old Testament* 35, no. 4 (2011): 417-433. This parallel seems weak insofar as the naked ones don't do the cursing but receive the curse in Genesis 3.

In Genesis 3, Adam and Eve's awareness of their nakedness requires that they be covered. Nudity should be avoided according to several passages (e.g., Exod 20:26; 28:42), and covering someone else's nakedness is extoled in other passages (e.g., Ezek 16:7-8; 18:7, 16). We need be careful not to superimpose our comfort level with seeing people's nakedness back into this account.

4. Paternal Incest. Since "seeing" and "uncovering" someone's nakedness serve as euphemisms for intercourse elsewhere in Torah (e.g., Lev 20:17), it is quite possible that Ham has committed some sort of sexual impropriety against his father.[151] This interpretation explains why Noah was furious with Ham once he realized what he had "done to him" and proceeded to curse his progeny. That the cursed progeny happens to be the ancestor of the sexually immoral Canaanites means that this account functions as an etiology of the residents of Canaan. Israel's sexual code, in Leviticus 18, begins by instructing the Israelites not to "do as they do in the land of Canaan" (v. 3). Furthermore, Genesis 19:30-38 provides an unambiguous etiology of the Ammonites and Moabites, which involves Lot's daughters getting him drunk and having intercourse with him.

5. Maternal Incest. This position has many of the same strengths as the paternal incest position. It is made possible by the fact that, in Leviticus, a man who lays with another man's wife is said to have uncovered the man's nakedness, whether it's his father, uncle, or brother (20:11, 20-21). Unlike the paternal incest

---

[150] Odhiambo, "The Nature of Ham's Sin," 162-165.

[151] While some interpreters see the core problem as incest and disrespect for one's father, Gershon Hepner faults Ham for violating the Holiness Code laws about homosexuality (Lev 18:22; 20:13). "The Depravity of Ham and the Tower of Babel Echo Contiguous Laws of the Holiness Code," *Estudios Biblicos* 61 (2003): 85-131.

theory, this position explains both why Noah undressed himself and why he cursed Canaan and not Ham. According to Bergsma and Hahn, Noah was naked because he was attempting to procreate with his wife. He apparently drank too much and wasn't able to perform. When Ham realizes this, he strives to assert his predominance in the family (like Reuben later does in Gen 35:22) by sleeping with his mother.[152] Because she ends up conceiving, Noah curses the son that is born of this illicit union. I would add to this theory that Noah may not have born additional children because he couldn't bring himself to having intercourse with his wife after Ham had slept with her.[153]

We cannot know for sure which of these scenarios the author had in mind. Yet given the artful and deliberate way previous sections of Genesis have been woven together, it seems likely that the author is making strategic use of subtle intertextual references to convey sensitive information. This lends considerable support to the last two options.

---

[152] Embry discounts this position, following Jacob Milgrom, because the phrase "uncover nakedness" applies to every situation except adultery ("The 'Naked Narrative' from Noah to Leviticus," 418-19). They deduce from this that it cannot apply to a married woman. Since Noah was married, this phrase cannot refer to maternal incest. However, Lev 18:7 seems to indicate that this is possible: "You shall not uncover the nakedness of your father, which is the nakedness of your mother; she is your mother, you shall not uncover her nakedness."

[153] The prophet Amos decried the practice of a father and son sleeping with the same woman (Amos 2:7). In Deut 24:1-4 a man who divorces his wife and forces her to marry and have intercourse with another man is forbidden from taking his wife back even if the second husband dies, since the woman has become "defiled." Perhaps Noah refused to sleep with his wife for similar reasons.

[154] See Graydon F. Snyder and Kenneth M. Shaffer, "On Racism," *Brethren Life & Thought* (Fall 2009): 55-60; and Edwin M. Yamauchi, "The Curse of Ham," *Criswell Theological Review* 6, no. 2 (Spr 2009): 45-60.

Recent scholars tend to agree, however, that the curse on Canaan has been grossly misappropriated to support African slavery.[154] It is more accurate to say that this passage anticipates that Shem will be the progenitor of the nation of Israel and Canaan the progenitor of the inhabitants of the Promised Land, whom Shem's descendants will dispossess and in some cases enslave. This curse is not about race as much as place. It is certainly not about skin color. If it were, Noah would not have cursed Canaan, but one of Ham's other three sons—each of whom was directly associated with Africa: Egypt, Cush (Ethiopia, Nubia, Sudan), and Put (Libya).

Back to the Narrative

The vineyard of Noah was clearly intended to echo the garden of Eden. What could this mean for the unfolding narrative? Noah's fall does more than repeat an earlier event with different characters. It also propels the storyline forward. The original Fall created a crisis in God's creation: How will God respond to human sinfulness? The chapter 9 fall account creates a crisis in the new creation: What will God do now, since he denied himself the option of washing away human wickedness with another flood?

In placing this troubling account immediately after the flood, the Genesis author thrusts readers back in the middle of the next crisis. But it's still early. Perhaps Noah's family can turn things around. Perhaps wickedness won't escalate like it did with Cain, Lamech, and the sons of God. Readers will have to wait until chapter 11 because, in dramatic fashion, the final author or editor of Genesis slows things down a bit by introducing another genealogy. As we might expect, this genealogy is no mere filler. It provides valuable information for fully appreciating the next big event in the unfolding primeval drama.

10:1-32 The Dispersion of Noah's Sons

We learned from Genesis 5 that genealogies contain a host of valuable information. Noah's genealogy in this chapter is no exception. Once again, we will home in on its core message and function by identifying formal elements unique to this genealogy and by exploring the significance of various deviations from the norm.

Form

Structure-wise this genealogy is broken into three sections corresponding to Noah's three sons. Unlike other genealogies, we receive no information concerning how long people lived or how old they were when their first son was born. Wives and daughters are left out completely. Each section lists all of Noah's son's sons. Then, following no consistent pattern, it lists further descendants of some but not all of Noah's grandsons.

Excluding Noah and his sons, the number of people groups in this genealogy is 70. Throughout the Old Testament, this number symbolizes completeness (e.g., 2 Chron 36:21; Dan 9:24). In this context, it probably serves to emphasize that *all* the earth's inhabitants truly descended from Noah and his sons. Notably, toward the end of Genesis, Jacob's entire 70-member household goes with him to Egypt (46:27). As the new world's population derives from Noah and his sons, so the new set apart people of God derives from Jacob after whom the people of Israel are named.

Each section concludes by specifying the regions where these descendants settled and by noting that this list comprises the lands, languages, clans, and nations from each son (vv. 5, 20, 31). No other biblical genealogy does this. It is less a family tree and more an etiology of nations and tribal groups that occupy specific territories.[155] This is why Genesis 10 is often referred to as the "table of nations." It also accounts for why there are no females. The

---

[155] If it were a family tree, we'd know that it is incomplete. In vv. 25-29, we see the lineage of Eber. He has two sons: Peleg and Joktam. Joktam's 13 descendants are named and none of Peleg's sons are named. We know from 11:18 that Peleg had multiple sons and daughters.

list isn't about naming every child but identifying the ancestral root of each territory.

This twofold structure serves at least two purposes. First, in keeping the emphasis on the whole world descending from Noah's family, it follows that all peoples, linguistic groups, and nations may be traced back to one of the ark's passengers. Second, this genealogy sets up the Babel account in chapter 11, in which all people populate one city and speak one language until God intervenes by diversifying their speech.

In other words, Noah's descendants didn't immediately go about establishing a diverse array of competing nations. After the Babel fiasco, God prodded them in that direction. This raises the question as to how Genesis 10 and 11 relate to one another from a chronological perspective. A glance back to Genesis 1-2 is instructive. Chapter 1 gives the big picture of how the entire created order came to be. Then chapter 2 zooms in on the creation of humans and animals. In so doing, it puts flesh on the rather skeletal structure of chapter 1. Without it, we wouldn't know the intimate way God created humans and the careful thought he put into the marital relationship. Likewise, the genealogy in Genesis 10 leaves us assuming that humans naturally spread out into the diverse political and linguistic enclaves that populate the earth. Without chapter 11, we wouldn't know that diverse human languages constitute another strategic divine initiative.

Made for Community

We find here in this account the birth of numerous nations. Included in that is not only the diversity in languages but the accompanying cities ... Nineveh, Rehoboth-ir, Calah, and more. As we'll soon see in Genesis 11 God was the one behind the geographic dispersion of people which led to not only nation building, but city building as well. This goes back to the heart of the first few chapters of Genesis. Since God has existed since eternity past in community and has thus created us *Imago Dei* then we can see how culture, the birth of new nations, languages, and cities is

> thus a natural outflow of this. We were made for community. We were also made to create. This then ties into the "urban mandate" of Genesis 1:28 which is more than animal husbandry but leads to cities.
>
> *Sean Benesh*

Chapter 10 teaches us to interpret linguistic diversity as part and parcel of international diversity. Consequently, chapter 11 should not be reduced to divine discipline of one particularly prideful nation. For it is also God's way of populating this earth with a multiplicity of diverse nations. This insight is key to a missional reading of Genesis and a biblical view of nationhood.

Having established the default pattern of this particular genealogy, we are now positioned to identify deviations from the norm with regard to each of Noah's sons.

Japheth

Japheth's line is the most regular of the three. Many of the nations he spawned are recognizable. They are the most neutral clans in the Old Testament narrative. For the most part, his descendants live far away from the Promised Land and therefore seldom threatened the wellbeing of God's people around the time Genesis was written. They are associated with regions like Ionia (Javan), Asia Minor (Meshach and Tubal), Media (Madai), Thrace (Tiras), Scythia (Ashkenaz), Cyprus (Elishah), and territories as far West as Crete (Kittim), Rhodes (Rodanim), and Spain (Tarshish). They are associated with coastal regions in verse five because many of them were best reached by sailing ships across the Mediterranean Sea.

It is likely intentional that *seven* sons of Japheth are named, as well as *seven* grandsons. Seven is a positive number, and both generations beneath Japheth contain clusters of seven. This may reflect ancient Israel's unique perspective on distant nations. As far as foreigners go, God's people would have looked favorably upon them. From a missional perspective, they were precisely the folk that the Israelites hoped to bless someday in fulfillment of

God's promise to Abraham in 12:3 (cf. Ps 97:1; Isa 42:4-12; 66:19).[156]

Ham's Line

> **Genetic Code of Cities**
>
> It is interesting how the origins of cities act in a way of setting the genetic code and culture of the city for the rest of its days. New York City was established by Dutch immigrants where trade and economics was woven into the city's DNA from the beginning. Today New York City is still known for its global position as a financial hub. From the beginning cities like Babylon and nations listed in Ham's line were at odds with Israel and we see this storyline evident throughout the rest of Scripture.
>
> *Sean Benesh*

As we might expect, given the behavior of Ham and the curse on Canaan, we find quite different sentiments concerning Ham's descendants. They are a veritable "Who's Who" of Israel's worst enemies, including the Egyptians, Babylonians, Assyrians, Philistines, Arabs, and all the smaller nations that the Israelites had to drive out of the Promised Land (vv. 15-18). Further indictment is present in verse 19 where the author notes the migration of Canaanites in the direction of Sodom, Gomorrah, Admah, and Zeboiim—cities that God dramatically destroys because of their rampant wickedness (Gen 19; cf. Deut 29:23).

Ham's line also contains the most significant deviation from the standard genealogical form. The author's lengthy digression on the legacy of Nimrod, son of Cush, has provoked more scholarly discussion in recent years than any other figure in this genealogy. Though most of the cities associated with Nimrod are well-attested historically,

---

[156] The prophets still anticipated divine judgment on the wicked among the coastlands (e.g., Isa 59:18; Ezek 39:6).

the man himself is unknown in ancient Near Eastern literature, at least by the name Nimrod.

This hasn't prevented scholars from linking him to ancient Mesopotamian gods—like Marduk[157] and Ninurta[158]—and kings—like Hammurabi,[159] Sargon I,[160] or the Sargonid dynasty.[161] The case for Sargon I and perhaps his wider dynasty is quite compelling because it accounts for nearly all the details in verses 9-12. In Assyrian records, Sargon I is remembered as the first mighty warrior king to dominate southern Mesopotamia (~ 2300 BC). He rose to prominence as a cupbearer and became king of Kish, which may explain his connection to Cush. He later moved his capital to Accad and changed his title from "King of Kish" to "King of Sumer and Akkad."[162] His realm enveloped the land of Shinar, where he built the cities of Accad and Babylon. During his long, 56-year reign, he launched a successful northern campaign, conquering Mari, Ebla,

---

[157] Aron Pinker, "Nimrod Found?" *Jewish Biblical Quarterly* 26, no. 4 (1998): 237-245.

[158] Terry Fenton, "Nimrod's Cities: An Item from the Rolling Corpus," in *Genesis, Isaiah and Psalms: A Festschrift to honour Professor John Emerton for his Eightieth Birthday*, eds Katherine J. Dell, Graham Davies, and Yee Von Koh (Boston: Brill, 2010), 23-31; K. van der Toorn and P. W. van der Horst, "Nimrod Before and After the Bible," *Harvard Theological Review* 83, no. 1 (1990): 1-29.

[159] David S. Farkas, "In Search of the Biblical Hammurabi," *Jewish Biblical Quarterly* 39, no. 3 (2011): 159-164.

[160] Israel Knohl, "Nimrod, Son of Cush, King of Mesopotamia and the Dates of P and J," in Birkat *Shalom: Studies in the Bible, Ancient Near Eastern Literature, and Postbiblical Judaism; Present to Shalom M. Paul on the Occasion of his Seventieth Birthday*, ed. Chaim Cohen (Winona Lake, IN: Eisenbrauns: 2008), 45-52.

[161] Yigal Levin, "Nimrod the Mighty, King of Kish, King of Sumer and Akkad," *Vetus Testamentum* 52, no. 3 (2002): 350-366.

[162] Levin, "Nimrod the Mighty," 359-60.

Ashur, and Nineveh. What is more, at the time Genesis was written, Sargon II had successfully revived the Sargonid dynasty (Neo-Assyrian Empire) and built Dur-Sarukkin as the new capital. It is possible that the Babel account is polemically critiquing this building project and that Dur-Sarukkin is represented by Resen in 10:12.[163]

One weakness of the Sargon theory is his name. Yet this is not a deal breaker. The biblical author, who links Nimrod to the Babel building project in chapter 11, may have given him a symbolic name that fits his role in this narrative.[164] The builders of Babel rebelled against God's commission to multiply and fill the earth and strove to construct a centralized city in order to "make a *name*" for themselves (11:4). Because God didn't approve of this project, they are ironically never actually named in that account. The chapter 10 genealogy couldn't acknowledge Sargon by name because doing so would fulfill his rebellious objective and negate the censure of chapter 11. Instead, he receives the symbolic name Nimrod, which quite appropriately means "let us rebel." A symbolic name would also be more appropriate if Nimrod was meant to represent the wider Sargonid dynasty and not just one man.

---

[163] Resen is a small village that stands out like a sore thumb among the other major Assyrian capitals associated with Nimrod in Genesis 10. Dur-Sarukkin is the only Assyrian capital not listed, which makes sense because it wasn't built until long after the time of Sargon I. However, Resen is very close to the place where Sargon II built Dur-Sarukkin, so it is quite possible that the Genesis author chose Resen as a geographical place marker. This makes sense since the author goes out of his way to point out where this city is located. Otherwise, his readers would likely not have heard of it. Though Dur-Sarukkin is not located exactly between Nineveh and Calah, one passes through it when traveling the royal roads between these major cities. Cf. Victor Avigdor Hurowitz, "In Search of Resen (Genesis 10:12): Dur-Sarrukin?" in *Birkat Shalom: Studies in the Bible, Ancient Near Eastern Literature, and Postbiblical Judaism; Present to Shalom M. Paul on the Occasion of his Seventieth Birthday*, ed. Chaim Cohen (Winona Lake, IN: Eisenbrauns: 2008), 511-524.

[164] Knohl, "Nimrod, Son of Cush," 51.

The connection between Sargon and hunting is somewhat weak. Perhaps it goes without saying that mighty warriors have a penchant for hunting animals.[165] Or, perhaps, this is a deliberate addition of the Genesis author. The narrative has consistently drawn attention to and lamented the impact of human violence on animals. For ancient Israel, hunting was not a glorified occupation the way it was for the Assyrians. The only other hunter mentioned in Genesis is Esau (Gen 25:27), who was hardly a paragon of virtue.[166] That Nimrod was a mighty hunter "before the LORD" doesn't mean he had God's approval. It may simply be a way of asserting that Nimrod wasn't a god since anything "before" Israel's God cannot be a god.[167] Plus, the term translated "before" can also mean "against," "in opposition to," or literally "in God's face." It functions this way in the First Commandment: "You shall have no other gods *before me*" (Exod 20:3).

At the end of the day, immediate context should be decisive. In that regard—and this will be more evident after we discuss chapter 11—the strong links between Nimrod, Babel, and Israel's oppressors suggest that this phrase is not a compliment.[168]

---

[165] Knohl draws attention to an ancient Assyrian song in praise of a hunter king (51).

[166] Esau the hunter is contrasted with Jacob the non-hunter. More precisely, Genesis 25:27 describes Esau as a "knowing hunter" and Jacob as a "complete/healthy/civilized/guiltless tent-dweller." The sense of the word *tam*, which modifies Jacob as a tent-dweller is not clear, but it's connotations are one-sidedly positive, which is meant to contrast with Esau as a hunter. The NRSV and most other translations obscure this. For the remainder of the Old Testament, hunting is mostly a metaphor for people who devour other people (Lam 3:52; 4:18; Ezek 13:18-21; Mic 7:2). It is not depicted as a desirable career, normal way of gathering food, or serious means of communing with God's good creation. That said, Torah does not prohibit hunting. Rather, echoing Genesis 9:2-5, it requires anyone who hunts an animal to drain its blood (Lev 17:13).

[167] Fenton, "Nimrod's Cities," 25.

Shem's Line

Shem's lineage breaks form in a few ways. First, it draws special attention to Eber. He is the *seventh* descendent of Shem to be named. He is identified as the namesake of God's people in verse 21: "To Shem also, the father of *all the children of Eber*." From him, the Israelites received the name "Hebrews." Abram is introduced as a "Hebrew" in Genesis 14:1-3 and Jacob's entire family goes by that name in 43:32. Eber fathered two other exceptional persons in the Shem's lineage: Peleg and Joktan.

Peleg's name means division. In verse 25, we are told somewhat cryptically that "the earth was divided" in his day. This phrase could be interpreted in light of the events of this chapter, in which case it would refer to the division of all the earth's territories by Noah's sons.[169] Some creation science folk see it as referring to the continental drift, and others associate it with canal building projects that divided land in Mesopotamia.[170] The traditional—and most likely—explanation is that it refers to the division of all the peoples of the earth that happens at Babel in the next chapter.[171]

---

[168] Mary Katherine Y. H. Hom, "'...A Mighty Hunter before YHWH': Genesis 10:9 and the Moral-Theological Evaluation of Nimrod," *Vetus Testamentum* 60 (2010): 63-68.

[169] This view is reflected in Jubilees 8:7. Zvi Ron, "The Book of Jubilees and the Midrash Part 3: The Tower of Babel," *Jewish Bible Quarterly* 42, no. 3 (2014): 165-168.

[170] David M. Fouts names but does not espouse this view in "Peleg in Gen 10:25," *Journal of the Evangelical Theological Society* 41, no. 1 (Mar 1998): 17-21.

[171] Rabbis debated whether this division happened toward the end of Peleg's life, such that Eber miraculously prophesied this event, or whether it was happening already during the time of Peleg's birth. Zvi Ron, "Book of Jubilees," 165-66. The former theory is based on calculations of ages from the genealogy of ch. 11.

On the surface, there is nothing remarkable about Joktan's lineage. It simply lists 13 of his descendants much the same way it lists the descendants of others. Still, several subtle factors combine to make it stand out. We've already noted that he is the son of Eber, the namesake of the Hebrews. Both he and his brother Peleg had sons, but only Joktan's are listed in this genealogy. Peleg's descendants are discussed in the following chapter (11:18-19) in the context of the genealogy of Shem, which culminates in Terah's sons and, especially, Abram.

What does all of this mean? One of the consistent themes of Genesis is that the patriarchal promise is not passed along to *two* sons. When two sons are in the mix, one is chosen and the other is not. The chosen one is folded into the story of God's redemptive mission, and the unchosen son is blessed with about 12 sons and their story comes to an end with the naming of those sons.

We see this with Nahor whom God passed over in favor of Abram and then blessed with 12 sons (22:20-24).[172] We see this with Ishmael whom God passed over in favor of Isaac and then blessed with twelve sons (25:1-18). We see it with Esau whom God passed over in favor of Jacob and then blessed with eleven sons (36:40-43). But we see it first with Joktan whom God passed over in favor of Peleg and then blessed with thirteen sons (10:26-29). Indeed, Joktan has more descendants than anyone else in Noah's genealogy. The only person who comes close is Canaan who begets eleven clans (10:15-18). Perhaps God bestows a compensatory blessing upon Canaan as well, since he was cursed on account of his father's sin and not his own.

It is also interesting that Nahor and Ishmael have exactly twelve sons, which is an ideal number because it aligns with the number of sons God bestowed upon Jacob. God blesses Esau with one short of twelve, perhaps because he distained his birthright and sought to kill God's chosen

---

[172] Though Nahor and Abram had another brother, Haran died prematurely (11:28).

one. What, then, should we make of the fact that Joktan has one son too many? Should we think of him as also being less worthy of God's blessing? If Fred Blumenthal is right, perhaps we should. Having studied the meaning of the names of Joktam's sons, he concludes that they are associated with warfare, manmade religions, materialism, and death.[173] The only son whose name doesn't fit into one of these negative categories is his first son, Almoded. Though Blumenthal does not connect this to the theme of non-elect sons, it is interesting that Almoded means "overlooked." The first son of Jotkam symbolizes the overlooked nature of his lineage.

God's blessing on overlooked sons in Genesis is too consistent to ignore. It teaches an important lesson about election and grace. God extends favor not only to his chosen people, but also to those who stand in close proximity to them. One wonders if the Apostle Paul had something like this in mind when he spoke about an unbelieving spouse being "sanctified" on account of being married to the believing spouse (1 Cor 7:14).

Finally, it is worth noting the strong parallels between Noah's lineage and that of Adam. Adam has three sons: one is good (Seth), one is evil (Cain), and one is neutral (Abel). Noah has three sons: one is good (Shem), one is evil (Ham), and one is neutral (Japheth). Both lines produce a standout villain: Adam has Lamech through Cain and Noah has Nimrod through Ham. Both Lamech and Nimrod are associated with cities that end up being dead ends as far as the future of the world is concerned. Lamech's city culminates in a violent world that God terminates with a flood, and God later shuts down Nimrod's city-building project by confusing its language and scattering its inhabitants. By way of contrast, Adam's son Seth gives birth to Noah through whom God leads humanity out of the sons of God debacle and subsequent flood, and Shem

---

[173] Fred Blumenthal, "Biblical Onomastics: What's in a Name," *Jewish Biblical Quarterly* 37, no. 2 (Apr-Jun 2009): 124-128.

gives birth to Abram through whom God leads humanity out of the Babel debacle, to which we now turn.

> ### The Overlooked of the City
>
> This notion of "God's blessing on overlooked sons in Genesis is too consistent to ignore" also applies on a practical level to cities and people within them. In many ministry circles there is a push to focus on cultural elites, culture shapers, and policymakers. The logic is that if these people are influenced by the gospel, then the rest of the culture will follow suit. In many cities where church planters are moving, it is mostly to plant churches in parts of the city with middle class and/or white-collar workers; the powerful and influential. This idea of "overlooked" is a great characteristic of where to live and whom to come alongside of to love. Whether these are cities or populations within cities, the overlooked are a good place to start ministry rather than giving them left-overs.
>
> *Sean Benesh*

11:1-9 The Dispersion of Nimrod's Sons

Perhaps no passage in Israel's primeval history is more overtly relevant to urban mission than Genesis 11:1-9. This pericope is often referred to as the "tower of Babel," but it would be more accurate to call it the "city of Babel." The tower is merely one feature of this city and arguably not the most important one. It is only mentioned in verses 4-5, whereas the fact that these people speak one language frames the entire pericope and is mentioned in verses 1, 6-7, and 9. Furthermore, God doesn't personally comment on the city's tower, but on its uniform speech (v. 6).

> ### Does God Condemn Cities?
>
> Building on Cain's construction of a city in chapter 4, some have used this passage to point out that God condemns cities. Here we have the first semi-detailed account of the construction process of building a city, even noting the materials used. Was God at odds with the idea of city building, or was there another motive for his actions?

Cultural Appreciation

This issue of language is trending in the numerous articles that have been written on this passage in recent years. Scholars are preoccupied with whether God's confusion of languages at Babel should be viewed as punitive, positive, or both.[174] Put differently, did God originally want humans to speak one language, but since they abused this privilege he had to mix them? Or did God desire the multiplicity of languages, but humans dragged their feet, so God intervened at Babel to get them moving?

> **The Language of the City**
>
> Cities are defined by their culture which is ultimately informed and influenced by language. How can we think of Paris without the French language? Tokyo without Japanese? Mexico City without Spanish? To truly get to know a city we need to immerse ourselves in the culture which its language reflects. To successfully live among a different people, we need to transition from tourist to resident. Language is key.
>
> *Sean Benesh*

Norwegian missiologist Hinne Wagenaar brings such questions into conversation with Lamin Sanneh's seminal missiological work, *Translating the Message*.[175] Sanneh distinguishes between mission by diffusion and mission by

---

[174] Of course, some scholars are still exploring standard questions pertaining to dating and historical reference points. E.g., Paul H. Seeley, "The Date of the Tower of Babel and Some Theological Implications," *Westminster Theological Journal* 63 (2001): 15-38; Paul T. Penley, "A Historical Reading of Genesis 11:1-9: The Sumerian Demise and Dispersion Under the UR III Dynasty," *Journal of the Evangelical Theological Society* 50, no. 4 (Dec 2007): 693-714.

[175] Lamin Sanneh, *Translating the Message: The Missionary Impact on Culture* (Marynoll, NY: Orbis Books 1989).

translation. The former transmits the gospel encased within the missionary's culture; the latter translates the gospel into the recipient's culture. Most missionaries now agree that translation is good and diffusion is bad. If cultural diversity is such a positive thing, it follows that the linguistic diversity that God incited at Babel is also a positive thing, and the cultural uniformity being pursued by the residents of Babel was the real problem.

Wagenaar argues this is how the original audience would have interpreted this story, albeit for different reasons. In their day, Babylon sought to subjugate all nations by imposing their language and culture on them. Of course, ruling elites typically frame their imperial ambition in ways that appeal to the masses. So, in Genesis 11:4, we read that the people hunkered down in this city so as not to be scattered across the earth with all the instability and uncertainties that would entail. Better to stick with the enemy they know. Yet God knows centralized domination when he sees it, so he thwarts the imperial elite and liberates the masses by confusing their speech.

Dispersal of Culture

While we may never uncover with absolute clarity the motives behind God's dispersal of populations and the diversity of languages and cultures, we can be confident that God initiated it. As in Genesis 4, Cain building a city coming on the heels of Cain murdering his brother does not then lead to the logical conclusion that all cities are cursed and an aberration. Origin stories are fraught with tension and the messiness of life. Abraham was promised a child but took matters into his own hands and had a child with his servant. He later lied repeatedly to save his life when he claimed Sarah was his sister. None of these threw off the notion that God was still at work, moving forward with his redemptive plan. The same can be said of some of the muddy roots of cities, culture, and languages.

Sean Benesh

For different reasons and with different nuances, the notion of Babel as both punishment and grace has been articulated by a diverse array of scholars, including theologians, linguists, and psychologists.[176] Yet this growing uniformity of interpretation is threatened, Babel-like, by the provocative thesis of Theodore Hiebert.[177] He challenges the both/and model by burying the punishment motif all together. The way he sees it, the people of Babel were not being prideful, challenging God's supremacy, building an oppressive regime, or trying to control the masses.

Consider Hiebert's evidence. No king is mentioned. Their stated motive is to avoid being scattered. A tower reaching into the sky was normal, not an affront to God. Acquiring a good name was a noble endeavor, not an act of hubris. Most importantly, God expresses no concern about the size of the city or the direction of its tower. His only stated

---

[176] Nancy L. deClaissé-Walford, "God Came Down...and God Scattered: Acts of Punishment or Acts of Grace?" *Review and Expositor* 103 (Spr 2006): 403-417; Marianne Moyaert, "A 'Babelish' World (Genesis 11:1-9) and its Challenge to Cultural-Linguistic Theory," *Horizons* 36, no. 2 (2009): 215-34; Allen S. Maller, "The City of Babel and Its Tower," *Jewish Biblical Quarterly* 40, no. 3 (2012): 171-173; Paul Cantz and Mirel Castle, "A Psycho-Biblical Response to Death Anxiety: Separation and Individuation Dynamics in the Babel Narrative," *Journal of Psychology & Theology* 41, no. 4 (2013): 327-339; Byron L. Sherwin, "The Tower of Babel in Eliezer Ashkenazi's *Sefer Ma'aseh Hashem*," *Jewish Biblical Quarterly* 42, no. 2 (2014): 83-88; Lyle Eslinger, "The Enigmatic Plurals like 'One of Us' (Genesis I 26, III 22, and XI 7) in Hyperchronic Perspective," *Vetus Testamentum* 56, no. 2 (2006): 172-184; Sheila Tuller Keiter, "Outsmarting God: Egyptian Slavery and the Tower of Babel," *Jewish Biblical Quarterly* 41, no 3 (2013): 200-204.

[177] Theodore Hiebert, "The Tower of Babel and the Origin of the World's Cultures," *Journal of Biblical Literature* 126 (2007): 29-58.

[178] John T. Strong, "Shattering the Image of God: A Response to Theodore Hiebert's Interpretation of the Story of the Tower of Babel," *Journal of Biblical Literature* 127, no. 4 (2008): 625-634; and André Lacocque, "Whatever Happened in the Valley of Shinar? A Response to Theodore Hiebert," *Journal of Biblical Literature* 128, no. 1 (2009): 29-41.

concern is their uniform speech. It wasn't his design and it's not inherently sinful, but given what they have accomplished already, it's quite possible they will never move beyond their single tongue and culture. So God nudged them forward by confusing their languages. What we have, then, is a simple account of the origin of diverse cultures. Such diversity is God's will for his world. This isn't like other crime-and-punishment accounts in early Genesis, and we shouldn't impose that framework upon it.

Hiebert's thesis was provocative enough to receive two formal rebuttals.[178] Though they haven't quite defeated his position, they've exposed critical weaknesses. If Genesis 11:1-9 existed by itself as an ancient story by some random ancient Mesopotamian clan, his interpretation would be perfectly defensible. The problem is that it exists among the Scriptures of the ancient Hebrews as part of a wider narrative replete with intertextual references that speak to their specific concerns as a people. The question interpreter's must answer is not, "Can this pericope be interpreted as saying what Hiebert proposes?" but "Would the original audience who received this text in the context of Genesis and as a part of their national self-understanding have interpreted it the way he proposes?"

For instance, would sixth century Israelites have interpreted the location of Shinar and naming of Babel as a mere reference to the cradle of civilization? Or, would they think of Babylon the way their prophets did—as an oppressive power that crushes cities, defiles temples, exiles prominent citizens, and otherwise ravages people (e.g., Hab 1-2). Remember also that in Genesis itself, God calls Abraham to leave Babylon and then, a few chapters later, Abraham has to rescue his nephew from a king of Shinar's periodic raids (14:1). Though Hiebert has closed the lid on interpretations of Babel as entirely punitive, it strains credulity to think an etiological text about Israel's arch-nemesis has absolutely no polemical intent.

Imperial Critique

The case for a polemical reading is strengthened when we locate the Babel story within the narrative trajectory that extends through Israel's primeval history. We've already observed that the genealogy in chapter 10 identifies Nimrod as the king who ruled the region of Shinar and the city of Babel (v. 10). This is clearly the same city discussed in chapter 11. The collective portrait of Babel in chapters 10 and 11 calls to mind the sons of God incident in 6:1-4. In chapter 10, Babel's founder, Nimrod, is called a *geber* or "mighty man." In chapter 11, the inhabitants of his city seek to make a *shem* or "name" for themselves. These terms are all we have in the brief description of the Nephilim in 6:4. They were "mighty men" of "name" whose service to the sons of God filled the world with violence. This continues the trajectory of the first city, Cain's city, where violence escalated under Lamech.

Playing it forward, then, we have a narrative in which Cain kills his brother, Lamech escalates violence in the first city, and warlords make violence so pervasive that God elects to flood the earth. Afterward, God promises not to flood the earth again, which leaves readers wondering how humanity will handle their new start. God asserts that people haven't changed. This is confirmed by power moves and sexual abuse in Noah's family, and now it escalates with the first postdiluvian city whose founders are described in ways reminiscent of the Nephilim.

The Babel account also anticipates Hebrew enslavement in Egypt. The residents of Babel say, "Come, let us make bricks" (v. 3) and "come, let us build ourselves a city" (v. 4).[179] Then God fittingly responds, "Come, let us go down, and confuse their languages" (v. 7). This is the final enigmatic use of the divine plural, and it reveals a pattern. In its only three uses in Scripture, all contained in the primeval history, the divine plural serves to delineate boundaries

---

[179] Keiter, "Outsmarting God," 200-204.

between God and humans.[180] In 1:26, God says, "let *us* make humankind in our image," indicating that humans are likened to God in a way that sets them apart from the rest of the created order, over which humans are uniquely given dominion. After humans abuse that dominion, by eating from the tree of knowledge, which represents divine limitations on their dominion, God says, "See, the man has become like one of *us*, knowing good and evil" (3:22). So God separates them from the tree of life so they will not live forever.

In 11:7, humans are pushing the divine boundary again. It is tempting to attribute this to the fact that they are building a tower "into the heavens." But a high reaching tower likely means nothing more than they are trying to build an impressive city. "Into the heavens" didn't mean into God's dwelling place, but into the sky, which would be impressive enough to earn them a name. In like manner, ancient Babylonians boasted of ziggurats reaching into the heavens.[181] Another option is that they are abusing their dominion on loan from God, like they did with the tree of life. Rather than obey God's command to be fruitful and multiply, they stay in one place and build an empire where the ruling elite monopolize the dominion God gave all people by dominating the masses.

This kind of dominion anticipates Egypt. The next time humans say, "Come, let us" it is in Egypt. Fearing that the multiplying Israelites are becoming a threat, the Egyptian rulers say, "Come, let us deal shrewdly with them" (Exod 1:10). They then put them to slave labor, building impressive cities with "brick and mortar" (1:14). Baking, transporting, and building with baked brick and mortar was the most primitive form of oppressive factory work, especially in the hot Egyptian sun. It is difficult to imagine

---

[180] Eslinger, "The Enigmatic Plurals," 172-184.

[181] Hiebert, "The Tower of Babel," 37.

the original audience not seeing Babel as foreshadowing Egypt and ultimately Babylon.

International Accountability

None of this means that the scattering of languages is purely punitive. It constitutes divine judgment upon humans lording over other humans in imperial fashion, it affirms cultural diversity, and it creates a plurality of competing political powers which God uses to keep violence, wickedness, and imperialism in check. Scholars have yet to fully appreciate this last point. Consider the evidence. When rulers lived exceedingly long lives and oppressed and dominated the earth, God responded by limiting human lifespans, flooding the earth, and beginning anew. We see in the genealogy to follow (11:10-26) that shortened lifespans had kicked in by the time of Peleg, when the earth was divided. If a long reigning king cannot give humans lasting stability and fame, then perhaps a great fortified city could. As much as humans didn't like being dominated, like Cain they feared the vulnerability of being isolated and defenseless. So wannabe kings built a following by appealing to the wider citizenry's sense of self-preservation and self-advancement. As short-lived humans, they couldn't personally guarantee lasting stability and prosperity, but their institutions would.

This is precisely the point where an empire-critical reading dovetails with a more charitable, safe-haven reading. Empire builders didn't think of themselves as being wicked, and they seldom start out that way. Rulers unite the masses by promising them a better life. Like Jesus says about Gentile rulers, they are viewed as benefactors (Luke 22:25). But God knew how evil the human heart remained. A large, strongly fortified city with noble aspirations is a ticking time bomb. Human wickedness and avarice eventually follows and benefactors become oppressors. The Egyptians started out providing food and land for grateful Israelites, but they ended up enslaving and exterminating them. The stronger an empire becomes, the more oppressive they become and the harder they are to resist.

This is what leads to the flood. To assure that something like the flood need not happen again, God intervenes with his final strategic initiative. In diversifying languages, God fosters a sprawling array of diverse cultures and civilizations that citizens would grow to love and strive to protect. They won't want some other civilization to march in and impose their own language and culture. In dispersing the builders of Babel, God creates a multiplicity of nations. This is precisely why the genealogy that sets up the Babel account repeatedly asserts itself as a genealogy of diverse languages, clans, territories, and nations (10:5, 20, 31). More specifically, it is the genealogy of the specific nations God uses throughout Israelite history as his instruments to advance his purposes, keep other nations in check, and even punish his own set-apart people. God uses Assyria to punish Israel, Babylon to punish Assyria, Persia to punish Babylon, Greece to punish Persia, and eventually Rome to punish Greece. To this day, God still uses the diversity of nations to keep various nations in check.

With this wide network of competing national egoisms in place, God would never have to flood the whole earth again. By separating them culturally and geographically, God can isolate particularly wicked nations, contain their wickedness, and deal with them one at a time—usually with the help of other self-interested nations who will feel threated by their growing wickedness. Hitler's Germany is an apt modern example. Sodom and Gomorrah is an ancient one. Though God ended up destroying the latter with sulfur and fire (ch. 18), it is worth noting that a federation of kings from the region of Babylon came earlier to subdue them (ch. 14)—but Abraham got involved for the sake of Lot and they were at least partially restored. One wonders if God would have destroyed those cities had Abraham not meddled, which only happened because he disobeyed God by bringing Lot with him to the Promised Land in the first place (12:1).

Grasping the significance of this global plurality of national powers is critical to the self-understanding of Israel and the church. These powers serve God's purpose of giving structure to society, punishing crime, and securing borders. When they do their job correctly, their people live in peace, and God's people can peacefully carry out their specific mission. When they don't, everything is disrupted, including the church's work. This is why the apostles instructed the early church to submit to and pray for governing authorities and warned them not to interfere with their work (Rom 13:1-7; 1 Tim 2:1-4; 1 Pet 2:13-17).

There's a great temptation for God's people to wield imperial power and serve as God's instrument of judging wickedness and the nations. Ancient Israelites wanted a king like the nations, but God told them they would only regret it, which they did. Jesus' disciples kept clamoring for power by asking to occupy prominent seats at Jesus's left and right, but Jesus said they would be servants rather than rule like the Gentiles. Unfortunately, after Jesus built his church as a non-territorial kingdom in contrast to the kingdoms of this world, the fourth century church gave in to the temptation to merge with the Roman Empire. But this is not the mission or posture to which God has called his people. God called them out of Babylon in Abraham's time and out of Egypt in Moses' time for a reason. He separated them out precisely because the way empires wield power is bad for humanity, even though it is useful for keeping others like them in check. More importantly, God wanted to use his people to be a blessing to *all nations* according to God's specific vision for human thriving.

By God's providential design, a plurality of nations serves to make this world a better place by promoting good and restraining evil among those who don't know him. The church, on the other hand, doesn't exist to make this world a better place, but to be the better place God has established in this world through Jesus.[182] We don't exist to manage or even coach the kingdoms of this world; we exist

---

[182] This is the core thesis of my book *Endangered Gospel: How Fixing the World is Killing the Church* (Eugene, OR: Cascade Books, 2016).

to embrace, display, and proclaim the kingdom that God brought through Jesus. God doesn't want his people to control the nations, but to offer them inclusion into God's alternative politics. God extends this offer as a gift that all people are free to accept or reject. His people must not compromise that God-given freedom by imposing it on the world with noble intentions or by naively, indeed rebelliously, striving to transform the fading kingdoms of this world into the everlasting kingdom of God.

Having established this world-preserving plurality of nations, the primeval narrative comes to an end. God's final strategic initiative to curb human wickedness and violence is in place. His next initiative won't focus on curtailing wicked living, but on exemplifying right living in God's good creation. The author transitions to this narrative by providing another genealogy.

God's Alternative Politics

The practical implications from this section are manifold. Reading through this section alone bears witness of the missiological ramifications of where and how God's people live life under the Kingdom of God in cities. In a world marked by ongoing urbanization, a wonderful diversity of culture and languages, and the mixed bag of the health and unhealth of cities, provides the perfect place for God's people to live out and display to their urban neighbors "inclusion into God's alternative politics." We are called to embody the good news of the counter-culture Kingdom of God. It is most exquisite in cities because of the size, scope, and diversity.

Sean Benesh

11:10-26 Shem's Son to Terah's Sons

Genealogy of Life

Here we encounter the final genealogy of the primeval prologue. Formally, it has a lot in common with Adam's genealogy. In fact, it follows the same exact pattern, save for the ending refrain, "and he died." This refrain was significant to the message of Genesis 5 insofar as it emphasized that disobeying God's command not to eat the forbidden fruit would lead to death, contrary to the serpent's claim.

Interestingly, chapter 5 ended in the middle of Noah's genealogical entry. It notes how old he was when he had his three sons, and then it ends. This sets up the events leading to the flood and the prominent role that Noah and his sons play in it. But unlike Enoch, Noah's genealogy ultimately ended in death. Immediately after the narrative about Noah and his sons, we have the completion of Noah's personal genealogy following the same form as chapter 5's genealogy of death: "After the flood Noah lived three hundred fifty years. All the days of Noah were nine hundred fifty years; *and then he died*" (9:28-29).

Now Shem's genealogy omits the line about death. This could simply mean that this chapter lacks the death verifying agenda of chapter 5. But the fact that it otherwise mirrors the form in chapter 5 and not the rest of the genealogies in Genesis (Nahor 22:20-24; Ishmael 25:12-17; Esau 36:1-43) suggests that the genealogies of chapter 5 and 11 are conceptually linked. That being the case, we might refer to Shem's genealogy as the genealogy of life. With the birth of Shem's great descendant Abram, a new chapter begins in world history: the life of God's set apart people.

It is evident that the birth of Abram signifies a new chapter in world history since only the verse about his birth deviates from the form of Shem's genealogy (11:26). Abram's name in particular does not stick out, but his father's entry does. All other entries name only one son and then conclude by noting how long the father lives after that son and the fact that he had additional sons and daughters. Terah's entry names three sons and then abruptly ends. The identification of three sons parallels Adam and Noah, both of whom had three sons and both of whom signaled a new era in world history.

Declining Ages

Aside from the missing death refrain, the only remarkable feature of Shem's genealogy is the numbers themselves. I am not referring to the sexagesimal numbering system that likely influenced the specific numbers chosen.[183] I am referring to the descending trend in the size of the numbers. Earlier, God stated he would limit lifespans to 120 (6:3). This genealogy shows that God meant what he said. Like his word about death, it took a while for the consequences to kick in, and the proof was contained in a genealogy. The following chart provides the age when each descendant bore his firstborn son, how long he lived afterward, and the total years he lived, which we calculated mathematically since the text does not say.[184]

---

[183] For detailed analysis of the actual numbers, see Dwight Wayne Young, "The Step-down to Two Hundred in Genesis 11, 10-25," *Zeitschrift für die alttestamentliche Wissenschaft* 116 (2004): 323-333.

[184] I placed in brackets all the numbers that are not actually in the genealogy and have been either calculated mathematically or imported from somewhere else in Genesis.

	Year of Firstborn	Additional Years	Total Years
Shem	100	500	[600]
Arpachshad	35	403	[438]
Shelah	30	403	[433]
Eber	34	430	[464]
Peleg	30	209	[239]
Reu	32	207	[239]
Serug	30	200	[230]
Nahor	29	119	[148]
Terah	70	[135]	[205]
Abraham	[86 / 100]	[89 / 75]	[175]

Starting with Shem, who lives to 600, the ages consistently descend except for two men: Eber and Terah. Eber, we noted in chapter 10 was an exceptional figure after whom the Hebrew people were named and from whom was born Peleg, who may have been named after the division of Babel. Terah fathers Abram and initiates the Patriarchal journey from Babylon to the Promised Land.

Two other numbers are significant, Shem bears his first son at age 100 and Terah at age 70, both of which are idealized numbers, being multiples of seven and ten. Significantly, Abraham gives birth to Isaac, the son of the promise, at age 100, in contrast to Ishmael the unchosen son whom he fathered at a numerically insignificant age. Shem's lineage also reveals that Abraham is the tenth descendant of Noah, who himself was the tenth descendant of Adam. Significant people are clearly associated with significant numbers.

"Name's" Name

> **Names of Cities**
>
> In modern times, names don't carry as much weight as they once did when people lived out the meaning of their names. On the other hand, studying the history of the names of cities reveals much. Portland, Oregon derived its name from a coin flip by two of the city's founders. One was from Boston and the other from Portland, Maine. Whoever won the coin flip would be able to name this fledging city founded on the banks of the Willamette River in a clearing of trees. New York City was originally New Amsterdam as it was established by Dutch settlers. When the English took it over in 1664 they changed the name to New York to honor the Duke of York. The name for Tucson, Arizona derived from the Spanish version of an *O'Odham* word that meant "at the base of the black hill" which is precisely where the city was founded. Names have meaning and can reveal a rich and interesting history of the development of a city. What about your city?
>
> *Sean Benesh*

This genealogy bridges the narrative of Babel with the narrative of Abram's calling in chapter 12. It does so not only by connecting the ancestral dots from Shem to Abram, but also through the meaning of Shem's name. Shem's name literally means "name." In the Babel account, the builders sought to make a "name" for themselves, echoing the legacy of the Nephilim. God terminated those plans, just like he did the Nephilim. Then, in 12:2, God promises Abram that he will make him a great nation and make his "name" great. It is thus fitting that these two episodes are connected by the genealogy of the man named "Name."

The meaning for readers is simple: those who wish to be part of the new world God begins with Abram should act in such a way that God might give them a great name and should avoid striving to make a name for themselves.[185]

11:27-32 Terah's False Start

Terah's Lineage

The primeval prologue ends with the brief account of Terah. As previously noted, Terah had three sons—like Adam and Noah before him—indicating that a new epoch in world history is beginning with him. In this brief pericope, Abram does not stand out, except that his wife Sarai is barren, which is important for the forthcoming plot. Abram takes center stage in chapter 12. Everything that we learn about his brothers and his father in this pericope serves to set the stage for him.

Although Haran is listed last in verses 26-27, he is most likely Terah's firstborn son. This is not stated explicitly in the text, but Paul Kissling has argued persuasively that Abraham was second and Nahor third. He arrives at this conclusion by calculating the age when Terah had sons, the location where Haran died, the age when Terah died, the date when Abraham left Haran, and the fact that Nahor married Haran's daughter.[186] The theme of first and second sons becomes important from this point forward.

We learn three other things about Haran. He fathered Lot as well as two daughters, Milcah and Iscah. He died in Babylon (Ur of the Chaldees).[187] His father likely named

---

[185] My understanding of this important theme in Genesis was enriched by the fine paper of Natasha Smith, which was a finalist in the 2012 Stone-Campbell Conference undergraduate student paper competition. Her paper was titled, "Prerequisite of a Redemptive Nation: The Theme of Name in Genesis and Beyond."

[186] Kissling, *Genesis*, vol. 2, 62–64.

[187] This assumes the traditional location of Ur in southern Mesopotamia. Scholars have suggested that Urkesh, 100 miles east/northeast of Haran, is another possible location. Patricia Berlyn, "The Journey of Terah: To Ur-Kasdim or Urkesh?" *Jewish Biblical Quarterly* 33, no. 2 (2005): 73-80. This theory attempts to address passages that seem to suggest that Abram was born near the territory of

the city Haran after him. Haran is located approximately at the halfway point of the journey from Ur to Jerusalem, but well north of both. Geometrically speaking, Haran forms the top point of a triangle—northeast of Jerusalem and northwest of Ur.[188] Lot returns to the story in chapter 12 when Abram chooses to bring him along to Canaan—a choice that complicates things for Abram. Milcah marries Abram's younger brother Nahor and is the grandmother of Rebekah who later becomes the wife of Abram's son Isaac (ch. 24).

> **Mobility at God's Nudging**
>
> There have been several times in my life when I almost "got stuck." I felt the nudging of God to "go" but I was afraid, fearful of the unknown. In some cases, I was in a place I loved and was comfortable. In each case there was a desire welling up to stay and be comfortable with the familiar. This doesn't mean following God *always* necessitates mobility and rootlessness, but looking back, I see these as definitive crossroads in my life. I made the leap. It was challenging to say the least. While I may never know the full extent of what transpired, I do know this ... my life was dramatically changed.
>
> *Sean Benesh*

Terah's Incomplete Journey

As far as a missional reading is concerned, the most noteworthy aspect of this pericope is the fact that Terah leaves Ur, with Abram, Lot, and Sarai, and heads *to Canaan*. This is significant because, in chapter 12, God calls Abram to leave his land and family behind to go to the land of Canaan (vv. 1-7). Since every word has been integral to the unfolding plot of the primeval story, this assertion raises the possibility that God had originally

---

Haran (e.g., Gen 24:2).

[188] It's about 700 miles from Ur to Haran and 550 miles from Haran to central Canaan. Berlyn, "The Journey of Terah," 77-78.

called Terah to be his chosen man to found a great nation that will be a blessing to all nations.[189]

For some reason, Terah elects to stay in Haran and never reaches his destination. Maybe he aged poorly and lacked the health and strength to continue. Maybe Haran proved to be a great and stable place to live, and he preferred the comfort that he knew above the uncertainty of Canaan. Perhaps Terah got hung up on the death of his firstborn. Perhaps the memory was too painful. If that were the case, it is all the more significant that the later test of Abraham's faith is surrendering the life of his own son, Isaac (ch. 22). In any event, it is quite possible that Haran had the faith to leave his home and begin the long journey, but not to complete it.

The text doesn't say for sure, but the story unfolds in such a way that commends it. When it was time for Abraham to find a wife for Isaac, he wanted him to marry a distant relative and not a Canaanite. Yet he refused to let Isaac go back to Haran, where Nahor's family lives, to acquire one. Abraham sent a servant on this mission because he didn't want Isaac to get stuck there like his grandfather. Likewise, when it was time for Isaac's son Jacob to acquire a wife, he is forced to visit Haran himself since his brother Esau wanted to kill him. As his story unfolds, Jacob gets stuck in Haran for over twenty years and has to deceive his father-in-law in order to escape. Given the way Haran functions in the lives of Isaac and Jacob, it is thus highly likely that the author regarded Terah's permanent layover in Haran as a negative thing.

This teaches us a valuable lesson about participation in God's mission. God will accomplish his world-saving mission one way or another. Anyone who wants to participate in that mission must remain faithful from beginning to end. Other offers will come our way—attractive opportunities to make a stable living for

---

[189] See Kissling, *Genesis*, vol 2, 64-65.

ourselves or to stay close to family. If we don't respond to God's invitation to a particular city, country, vocation, or church then God will raise up someone else in our place. As Mordecai famously told Esther, "if you keep silence at such a time as this, relief and deliverance will rise for the Jews from another quarter" (Esth 4:14).

Abraham, as we will see, responds faithfully and travels all the way. His journey is one of ups and downs. He has moments of great faith and little faith. But we all have the opportunity to become children of Abraham through faith in Jesus Christ because—unlike Terah—Abram didn't give up.

GENESIS 1-11 AND MISSION

The primeval prologue to the Bible story is a vital source for missiological reflection. It doesn't describe God's mission *per se*, but it sets forth the reasons for God's mission in this world and the global conditions within which God's mission takes place. Genesis 1-11 should not be reduced to the story of how God created a very good world and then humans soiled it with sin. Though that much is true, the story is much bigger and richer than that. It also involves the development of civilization, the rise of oppressive governing authorities, dramatic divine countermeasures to safeguard creation, human relapse into practices and structures of oppression, and additional divine countermeasures to protect God's perfect design for creation.

In short, it is a tug-of-war battle between creator and creatures with the future of world history on the line. From this turbulent history, we learn at least seven lessons that impact our understanding of Christian mission.

1. Since human sinfulness impacts all creation in all of its relationships, God's saving mission seeks to bring restoration and reconciliation in all things. Individualistic and otherworldly agendas are therefore out of step with God's mission.

2. Since sin thoroughly corrupts the human heart, God's people will not be naïvely optimistic about our capacity for good and our ability to fix what we've broken in this world. For this world to be saved, God will have to take the initiative.

3. Since God has covenanted to safeguard all creatures and preserve this world's natural rhythms, God's people will strive to exemplify proper stewardship of God's good creation at all times. We won't just do so when it is politically and culturally trendy.

4. Since God has chosen to carry out specific tasks through a righteous remnant, God's people will humbly fulfill his indispensable role for us. We must seek first

God's righteousness and focus on his will, especially when no one else does.

5. Since God uses a global network of nations to keep order and peace in the world, God's people will trust that God is at work in ways that are beyond our purview and calling. We must avoid usurping or even coveting responsibility for his wider work.

6. Since God squelched humanity's homogenizing impulse by fostering linguistic and cultural diversity, God's people must never erase cultural differences in the name of efficiency, safety, or unity. Our witness must respect all divinely ordained diversity.

7. Since God has affirmed his original intentions for creation time after time, God's people will inhabit this world in ways that exemplify those intentions. We must remember that God's ways always align with the grain of the universe.

These lessons are, of course, only *the Beginning*.

www.ingramcontent.com/pod-product-compliance
Lightning Source LLC
Chambersburg PA
CBHW061302110426
42742CB00012BA/2022